NoSQL Distilled

NoSQL Distilled

A Brief Guide to the Emerging World of Polyglot Persistence

Pramod J. Sadalage
Martin Fowler

✦Addison-Wesley

Upper Saddle River, NJ • Boston • Indianapolis • San Francisco
New York • Toronto • Montreal • London • Munich • Paris • Madrid
Capetown • Sydney • Tokyo • Singapore • Mexico City

Many of the designations used by manufacturers and sellers to distinguish their products are claimed as trademarks. Where those designations appear in this book, and the publisher was aware of a trademark claim, the designations have been printed with initial capital letters or in all capitals.

The authors and publisher have taken care in the preparation of this book, but make no expressed or implied warranty of any kind and assume no responsibility for errors or omissions. No liability is assumed for incidental or consequential damages in connection with or arising out of the use of the information or programs contained herein.

For information about buying this title in bulk quantities, or for special sales opportunities (which may include electronic versions; custom cover designs; and content particular to your business, training goals, marketing focus, or branding interests), please contact our corporate sales department at corpsales@pearsoned.com or (800) 382–3419.

For government sales inquiries, please contact governmentsales@pearsoned.com.

For questions about sales outside the U.S., please contact international@pearsoned.com.

Visit us on the Web: informit.com/aw

Library of Congress Cataloging-in-Publication Data

Sadalage, Pramod J.
  NoSQL distilled : a brief guide to the emerging world of polyglot
persistence / Pramod J Sadalage, Martin Fowler.
     p. cm.
  Includes bibliographical references and index.
  ISBN 978-0-321-82662-6 (pbk. : alk. paper) -- ISBN 0-321-82662-0 (pbk. :
alk. paper) 1. Databases--Technological innovations. 2. Information
storage and retrieval systems. I. Fowler, Martin, 1963- II. Title.
  QA76.9.D32S228 2013
  005.74--dc23

ISBN-13: 978-0-321-82662-6
ISBN-10: 0-321-82662-0
Text printed in the United States on recycled paper at RR Donnelley in Crawfordsville, Indiana.
Fifth printing, August 2015

For my teachers Gajanan Chinchwadkar,
Dattatraya Mhaskar, and Arvind Parchure. You
inspired me the most, thank you.
—Pramod

For Cindy
—Martin

Contents

Preface

We've spent some twenty years in the world of enterprise computing. We've seen many things change in languages, architectures, platforms, and processes. But through all this time one thing has stayed constant—relational databases store the data. There have been challengers, some of which have had success in some niches, but on the whole the data storage question for architects has been the question of which relational database to use.

There is a lot of value in the stability of this reign. An organization's data lasts much longer than its programs (at least that's what people tell us—we've seen plenty of very old programs out there). It's valuable to have a stable data storage that's well understood and accessible from many application programming platforms.

Now, however, there's a new challenger on the block under the confrontational tag of NoSQL. It's born out of a need to handle larger data volumes which forced a fundamental shift to building large hardware platforms through clusters of commodity servers. This need has also raised long-running concerns about the difficulties of making application code play well with the relational data model.

The term "NoSQL" is very ill-defined. It's generally applied to a number of recent nonrelational databases such as Cassandra, Mongo, Neo4J, and Riak. They embrace schemaless data, run on clusters, and have the ability to trade off traditional consistency for other useful properties. Advocates of NoSQL databases claim that they can build systems that are more performant, scale much better, and are easier to program with.

Is this the first rattle of the death knell for relational databases, or yet another pretender to the throne? Our answer to that is "neither." Relational databases are a powerful tool that we expect to be using for many more decades, but we do see a profound change in that relational databases won't be the only databases in use. Our view is that we are entering a world of Polyglot Persistence where enterprises, and even individual applications, use multiple technologies for data management. As a result, architects will need to be familiar with these technologies and be able to evaluate which ones to use for differing needs.

Had we not thought that, we wouldn't have spent the time and effort writing this book.

This book seeks to give you enough information to answer the question of whether NoSQL databases are worth serious consideration for your future projects. Every project is different, and there's no way we can write a simple decision tree to choose the right data store. Instead, what we are attempting here is to provide you with enough background on how NoSQL databases work, so that you can make those judgments yourself without having to trawl the whole web. We've deliberately made this a small book, so you can get this overview pretty quickly. It won't answer your questions definitively, but it should narrow down the range of options you have to consider and help you understand what questions you need to ask.

Why Are NoSQL Databases Interesting?

We see two primary reasons why people consider using a NoSQL database.

- **Application development productivity.** A lot of application development effort is spent on mapping data between in-memory data structures and a relational database. A NoSQL database may provide a data model that better fits the application's needs, thus simplifying that interaction and resulting in less code to write, debug, and evolve.

- **Large-scale data.** Organizations are finding it valuable to capture more data and process it more quickly. They are finding it expensive, if even possible, to do so with relational databases. The primary reason is that a relational database is designed to run on a single machine, but it is usually more economic to run large data and computing loads on clusters of many smaller and cheaper machines. Many NoSQL databases are designed explicitly to run on clusters, so they make a better fit for big data scenarios.

What's in the Book

We've broken this book up into two parts. The first part concentrates on core concepts that we think you need to know in order to judge whether NoSQL databases are relevant for you and how they differ. In the second part we concentrate more on implementing systems with NoSQL databases.

Chapter 1 begins by explaining why NoSQL has had such a rapid rise—the need to process larger data volumes led to a shift, in large systems, from scaling vertically to scaling horizontally on clusters. This explains an important feature of the data model of many NoSQL databases—the explicit storage of a rich structure of closely related data that is accessed as a unit. In this book we call this kind of structure an *aggregate*.

Chapter 2 describes how aggregates manifest themselves in three of the main data models in NoSQL land: key-value ("Key-Value and Document Data Models," p. 20), document ("Key-Value and Document Data Models," p. 20), and column family ("Column-Family Stores," p. 21) databases. Aggregates provide a natural unit of interaction for many kinds of applications, which both improves running on a cluster and makes it easier to program the data access. Chapter 3 shifts to the downside of aggregates—the difficulty of handling relationships ("Relationships," p. 25) between entities in different aggregates. This leads us naturally to graph databases ("Graph Databases," p. 26), a NoSQL data model that doesn't fit into the aggregate-oriented camp. We also look at the common characteristic of NoSQL databases that operate without a schema ("Schemaless Databases," p. 28)—a feature that provides some greater flexibility, but not as much as you might first think.

Having covered the data-modeling aspect of NoSQL, we move on to distribution: Chapter 4 describes how databases distribute data to run on clusters. This breaks down into sharding ("Sharding," p. 38) and replication, the latter being either master-slave ("Master-Slave Replication," p. 40) or peer-to-peer ("Peer-to-Peer Replication," p. 42) replication. With the distribution models defined, we can then move on to the issue of consistency. NoSQL databases provide a more varied range of consistency options than relational databases—which is a consequence of being friendly to clusters. So Chapter 5 talks about how consistency changes for updates ("Update Consistency," p. 47) and reads ("Read Consistency," p. 49), the role of quorums ("Quorums," p. 57), and how even some durability ("Relaxing Durability," p. 56) can be traded off. If you've heard anything about NoSQL, you'll almost certainly have heard of the CAP theorem; the "The CAP Theorem" section on p. 53 explains what it is and how it fits in.

While these chapters concentrate primarily on the principles of how data gets distributed and kept consistent, the next two chapters talk about a couple of important tools that make this work. Chapter 6 describes version stamps, which are for keeping track of changes and detecting inconsistencies. Chapter 7 outlines map-reduce, which is a particular way of organizing parallel computation that fits in well with clusters and thus with NoSQL systems.

Once we're done with concepts, we move to implementation issues by looking at some example databases under the four key categories: Chapter 8 uses Riak as an example of key-value databases, Chapter 9 takes MongoDB as an example for document databases, Chapter 10 chooses Cassandra to explore column-family databases, and finally Chapter 11 plucks Neo4J as an example of graph databases. We must stress that this is not a comprehensive study—there are too many out there to write about, let alone for us to try. Nor does our choice of examples imply any recommendations. Our aim here is to give you a feel for the variety of stores that exist and for how different database technologies use the concepts we outlined earlier. You'll see what kind of code you need to write to program against these systems and get a glimpse of the mindset you'll need to use them.

A common statement about NoSQL databases is that since they have no schema, there is no difficulty in changing the structure of data during the life of an application. We disagree—a schemaless database still has an implicit schema that needs change discipline when you implement it, so Chapter 12 explains how to do data migration both for strong schemas and for schemaless systems.

All of this should make it clear that NoSQL is not a single thing, nor is it something that will replace relational databases. Chapter 13 looks at this future world of Polyglot Persistence, where multiple data-storage worlds coexist, even within the same application. Chapter 14 then expands our horizons beyond this book, considering other technologies that we haven't covered that may also be a part of this polyglot-persistent world.

With all of this information, you are finally at a point where you can make a choice of what data storage technologies to use, so our final chapter (Chapter 15, "Choosing Your Database," p. 147) offers some advice on how to think about these choices. In our view, there are two key factors—finding a productive programming model where the data storage model is well aligned to your application, and ensuring that you can get the data access performance and resilience you need. Since this is early days in the NoSQL life story, we're afraid that we don't have a well-defined procedure to follow, and you'll need to test your options in the context of your needs.

This is a brief overview—we've been very deliberate in limiting the size of this book. We've selected the information we think is the most important—so that you don't have to. If you are going to seriously investigate these technologies, you'll need to go further than what we cover here, but we hope this book provides a good context to start you on your way.

We also need to stress that this is a very volatile field of the computer industry. Important aspects of these stores are changing every year—new features, new databases. We've made a strong effort to focus on concepts, which we think will be valuable to understand even as the underlying technology changes. We're pretty confident that most of what we say will have this longevity, but absolutely sure that not all of it will.

Who Should Read This Book

Our target audience for this book is people who are considering using some form of a NoSQL database. This may be for a new project, or because they are hitting barriers that are suggesting a shift on an existing project.

Our aim is to give you enough information to know whether NoSQL technology makes sense for your needs, and if so which tool to explore in more depth. Our primary imagined audience is an architect or technical lead, but we think this book is also valuable for people involved in software management who want to get an overview of this new technology. We also think that if you're a developer who wants an overview of this technology, this book will be a good starting point.

We don't go into the details of programming and deploying specific databases here—we leave that for specialist books. We've also been very firm on a page limit, to keep this book a brief introduction. This is the kind of book we think you should be able to read on a plane flight: It won't answer all your questions but should give you a good set of questions to ask.

If you've already delved into the world of NoSQL, this book probably won't commit any new items to your store of knowledge. However, it may still be useful by helping you explain what you've learned to others. Making sense of the issues around NoSQL is important—particularly if you're trying to persuade someone to consider using NoSQL in a project.

What Are the Databases

In this book, we've followed a common approach of categorizing NoSQL databases according to their data model. Here is a table of the four data models and some of the databases that fit each model. This is not a comprehensive list—it only mentions the more common databases we've come across. At the time of writing, you can find more comprehensive lists at http://nosql-database.org and http://nosql.mypopescu.com/kb/nosql. For each category, we mark with italics the database we use as an example in the relevant chapter.

Our goal is to pick a representative tool from each of the categories of the databases. While we talk about specific examples, most of the discussion should apply to the entire category, even though these products are unique and cannot be generalized as such. We will pick one database for each of the key-value, document, column family, and graph databases; where appropriate, we will mention other products that may fulfill a specific feature need.

Data Model	Example Databases
Key-Value ("Key-Value Databases," p. 81)	BerkeleyDB
	LevelDB
	Memcached
	Project Voldemort
	Redis
	Riak
Document ("Document Databases," p. 89)	CouchDB
	MongoDB
	OrientDB
	RavenDB
	Terrastore
Column-Family ("Column-Family Stores," p. 99)	Amazon SimpleDB
	Cassandra
	HBase
	Hypertable
Graph ("Graph Databases," p. 111)	FlockDB
	HyperGraphDB
	Infinite Graph
	Neo4J
	OrientDB

This classification by data model is useful, but crude. The lines between the different data models, such as the distinction between key-value and document databases ("Key-Value and Document Data Models," p. 20), are often blurry. Many databases don't fit cleanly into categories; for example, OrientDB calls itself both a document database and a graph database.

Acknowledgments

Our first thanks go to our colleagues at ThoughtWorks, many of whom have been applying NoSQL to our delivery projects over the last couple of years. Their experiences have been a primary source both of our motivation in writing this book and of practical information on the value of this technology. The positive experience we've had so far with NoSQL data stores is the basis of our view that this is an important technology and a significant shift in data storage.

We'd also like to thank various groups who have given public talks, published articles, and blogs on their use of NoSQL. Much progress in software development gets hidden when people don't share with their peers what they've learned. Particular thanks here go to Google and Amazon whose papers on Bigtable and Dynamo were very influential in getting the NoSQL movement going. We also thank companies that have sponsored and contributed to the open-source development of NoSQL databases. An interesting difference with previous shifts in data storage is the degree to which the NoSQL movement is rooted in open-source work.

Particular thanks go to ThoughtWorks for giving us the time to work on this book. We joined ThoughtWorks at around the same time and have been here for over a decade. ThoughtWorks continues to be a very hospitable home for us, a source of knowledge and practice, and a welcome environment of openly sharing what we learn—so different from the traditional systems delivery organizations.

Bethany Anders-Beck, Ilias Bartolini, Tim Berglund, Duncan Craig, Paul Duvall, Oren Eini, Perryn Fowler, Michael Hunger, Eric Kascic, Joshua Kerievsky, Anand Krishnaswamy, Bobby Norton, Ade Oshineye, Thiyagu Palanisamy, Prasanna Pendse, Dan Pritchett, David Rice, Mike Roberts, Marko Rodriquez, Andrew Slocum, Toby Tripp, Steve Vinoski, Dean Wampler, Jim Webber, and Wee Witthawaskul reviewed early drafts of this book and helped us improve it with their advice.

Additionally, Pramod would like to thank Schaumburg Library for providing great service and quiet space for writing; Arhana and Arula, my beautiful daughters, for their understanding that daddy would go to the library and not take them along; Rupali, my beloved wife, for her immense support and help in keeping me focused.

Part I

Understand

Chapter 1

Why NoSQL?

For almost as long as we've been in the software profession, relational databases have been the default choice for serious data storage, especially in the world of enterprise applications. If you're an architect starting a new project, your only choice is likely to be which relational database to use. (And often not even that, if your company has a dominant vendor.) There have been times when a database technology threatened to take a piece of the action, such as object databases in the 1990's, but these alternatives never got anywhere.

After such a long period of dominance, the current excitement about NoSQL databases comes as a surprise. In this chapter we'll explore why relational databases became so dominant, and why we think the current rise of NoSQL databases isn't a flash in the pan.

1.1 The Value of Relational Databases

Relational databases have become such an embedded part of our computing culture that it's easy to take them for granted. It's therefore useful to revisit the benefits they provide.

1.1.1 Getting at Persistent Data

Probably the most obvious value of a database is keeping large amounts of persistent data. Most computer architectures have the notion of two areas of memory: a fast volatile "main memory" and a larger but slower "backing store." Main memory is both limited in space and loses all data when you lose power or something bad happens to the operating system. Therefore, to keep data around, we write it to a backing store, commonly seen a disk (although these days that disk can be persistent memory).

The backing store can be organized in all sorts of ways. For many productivity applications (such as word processors), it's a file in the file system of the operating system. For most enterprise applications, however, the backing store is a database. The database allows more flexibility than a file system in storing large amounts of data in a way that allows an application program to get at small bits of that information quickly and easily.

1.1.2 Concurrency

Enterprise applications tend to have many people looking at the same body of data at once, possibly modifying that data. Most of the time they are working on different areas of that data, but occasionally they operate on the same bit of data. As a result, we have to worry about coordinating these interactions to avoid such things as double booking of hotel rooms.

Concurrency is notoriously difficult to get right, with all sorts of errors that can trap even the most careful programmers. Since enterprise applications can have lots of users and other systems all working concurrently, there's a lot of room for bad things to happen. Relational databases help handle this by controlling all access to their data through transactions. While this isn't a cure-all (you still have to handle a transactional error when you try to book a room that's just gone), the transactional mechanism has worked well to contain the complexity of concurrency.

Transactions also play a role in error handling. With transactions, you can make a change, and if an error occurs during the processing of the change you can roll back the transaction to clean things up.

1.1.3 Integration

Enterprise applications live in a rich ecosystem that requires multiple applications, written by different teams, to collaborate in order to get things done. This kind of inter-application collaboration is awkward because it means pushing the human organizational boundaries. Applications often need to use the same data and updates made through one application have to be visible to others.

A common way to do this is **shared database integration** [Hohpe and Woolf] where multiple applications store their data in a single database. Using a single database allows all the applications to use each others' data easily, while the database's concurrency control handles multiple applications in the same way as it handles multiple users in a single application.

1.1.4 A (Mostly) Standard Model

Relational databases have succeeded because they provide the core benefits we outlined earlier in a (mostly) standard way. As a result, developers and database professionals can learn the basic relational model and apply it in many projects. Although there are differences between different relational databases, the core mechanisms remain the same: Different vendors' SQL dialects are similar, transactions operate in mostly the same way.

1.2 Impedance Mismatch

Relational databases provide many advantages, but they are by no means perfect. Even from their early days, there have been lots of frustrations with them.

For application developers, the biggest frustration has been what's commonly called the **impedance mismatch**: the difference between the relational model and the in-memory data structures. The relational data model organizes data into a structure of tables and rows, or more properly, relations and tuples. In the relational model, a **tuple** is a set of name-value pairs and a **relation** is a set of tuples. (The relational definition of a tuple is slightly different from that in mathematics and many programming languages with a tuple data type, where a tuple is a sequence of values.) All operations in SQL consume and return relations, which leads to the mathematically elegant relational algebra.

This foundation on relations provides a certain elegance and simplicity, but it also introduces limitations. In particular, the values in a relational tuple have to be simple—they cannot contain any structure, such as a nested record or a list. This limitation isn't true for in-memory data structures, which can take on much richer structures than relations. As a result, if you want to use a richer in-memory data structure, you have to translate it to a relational representation to store it on disk. Hence the impedance mismatch—two different representations that require translation (see Figure 1.1).

The impedance mismatch is a major source of frustration to application developers, and in the 1990s many people believed that it would lead to relational databases being replaced with databases that replicate the in-memory data structures to disk. That decade was marked with the growth of object-oriented programming languages, and with them came object-oriented databases—both looking to be the dominant environment for software development in the new millennium.

However, while object-oriented languages succeeded in becoming the major force in programming, object-oriented databases faded into obscurity. Relational databases saw off the challenge by stressing their role as an integration mechanism, supported by a mostly standard language of data manipulation (SQL) and a growing professional divide between application developers and database administrators.

Impedance mismatch has been made much easier to deal with by the wide availability of object-relational mapping frameworks, such as Hibernate and iBATIS that implement well-known mapping patterns [Fowler PoEAA], but the mapping problem is still an issue. Object-relational mapping frameworks remove

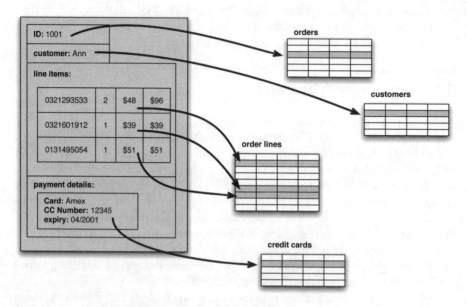

Figure 1.1 *An order, which looks like a single aggregate structure in the UI, is split into many rows from many tables in a relational database*

a lot of grunt work, but can become a problem of their own when people try too hard to ignore the database and query performance suffers.

Relational databases continued to dominate the enterprise computing world in the 2000s, but during that decade cracks began to open in their dominance.

1.3 Application and Integration Databases

The exact reasons why relational databases triumphed over OO databases are still the subject of an occasional pub debate for developers of a certain age. But in our view, the primary factor was the role of SQL as an integration mechanism between applications. In this scenario, the database acts as an **integration database**—with multiple applications, usually developed by separate teams, storing their data in a common database. This improves communication because all the applications are operating on a consistent set of persistent data.

There are downsides to shared database integration. A structure that's designed to integrate many applications ends up being more complex—indeed, often dramatically more complex—than any single application needs. Furthermore, should an application want to make changes to its data storage, it needs to coordinate with all the other applications using the database. Different applications have different structural and performance needs, so an index required by one application may cause a problematic hit on inserts for another. The fact that each application is usually a separate team also means that the database usually cannot trust applications to update the data in a way that preserves database integrity and thus needs to take responsibility for that within the database itself.

A different approach is to treat your database as an **application database**—which is only directly accessed by a single application codebase that's looked after by a single team. With an application database, only the team using the application needs to know about the database structure, which makes it much easier to maintain and evolve the schema. Since the application team controls both the database and the application code, the responsibility for database integrity can be put in the application code.

Interoperability concerns can now shift to the interfaces of the application, allowing for better interaction protocols and providing support for changing them. During the 2000s we saw a distinct shift to web services [Daigneau], where applications would communicate over HTTP. Web services enabled a new form of a widely used communication mechanism—a challenger to using the SQL with shared databases. (Much of this work was done under the banner of "Service-Oriented Architecture"—a term most notable for its lack of a consistent meaning.)

An interesting aspect of this shift to web services as an integration mechanism was that it resulted in more flexibility for the structure of the data that was being exchanged. If you communicate with SQL, the data must be structured as relations. However, with a service, you are able to use richer data structures with nested records and lists. These are usually represented as documents in XML or, more recently, JSON. In general, with remote communication you want to reduce the number of round trips involved in the interaction, so it's useful to be able to put a rich structure of information into a single request or response.

If you are going to use services for integration, most of the time web services—using text over HTTP—is the way to go. However, if you are dealing with highly performance-sensitive interactions, you may need a binary protocol. Only do this if you are sure you have the need, as text protocols are easier to work with—consider the example of the Internet.

Once you have made the decision to use an application database, you get more freedom of choosing a database. Since there is a decoupling between your internal database and the services with which you talk to the outside world, the outside world doesn't have to care how you store your data, allowing you to consider nonrelational options. Furthermore, there are many features of relational databases, such as security, that are less useful to an application database because they can be done by the enclosing application instead.

Despite this freedom, however, it wasn't apparent that application databases led to a big rush to alternative data stores. Most teams that embraced the application database approach stuck with relational databases. After all, using an application database yields many advantages even ignoring the database flexibility (which is why we generally recommend it). Relational databases are familiar and usually work very well or, at least, well enough. Perhaps, given time, we might have seen the shift to application databases to open a real crack in the relational hegemony—but such cracks came from another source.

1.4 Attack of the Clusters

At the beginning of the new millennium the technology world was hit by the busting of the 1990s dot-com bubble. While this saw many people questioning the economic future of the Internet, the 2000s did see several large web properties dramatically increase in scale.

This increase in scale was happening along many dimensions. Websites started tracking activity and structure in a very detailed way. Large sets of data appeared: links, social networks, activity in logs, mapping data. With this growth in data came a growth in users—as the biggest websites grew to be vast estates regularly serving huge numbers of visitors.

Coping with the increase in data and traffic required more computing resources. To handle this kind of increase, you have two choices: up or out. Scaling up implies bigger machines, more processors, disk storage, and memory. But bigger machines get more and more expensive, not to mention that there are real limits as your size increases. The alternative is to use lots of small machines in a cluster. A cluster of small machines can use commodity hardware and ends up being cheaper at these kinds of scales. It can also be more resilient—while individual machine failures are common, the overall cluster can be built to keep going despite such failures, providing high reliability.

As large properties moved towards clusters, that revealed a new problem—relational databases are not designed to be run on clusters. Clustered relational databases, such as the Oracle RAC Server, work on the concept of a shared disk subsystem. They use a cluster-aware file system that writes to a highly available disk subsystem—but this means the cluster still has the disk subsystem as a single point of failure. Relational databases could also be run as separate servers for different sets of data, effectively sharding ("Sharding," p. 38) the database. While this separates the load, all the sharding has to be controlled by the application which has to keep track of which database server to talk to for each bit of data. Also, we lose any querying, referential integrity, transactions, or consistency controls that cross shards. A phrase we often hear in this context from people who've done this is "unnatural acts."

These technical issues are exacerbated by licensing costs. Commercial relational databases are usually priced on a single-server assumption, so running on a cluster raised prices and led to frustrating negotiations with purchasing departments.

This mismatch between relational databases and clusters led some organization to consider an alternative route to data storage. Two companies in particular—Google and Amazon—have been very influential. Both were on the forefront of running large clusters of this kind; furthermore, they were capturing huge amounts of data. These things gave them the motive. Both were successful and growing companies with strong technical components, which gave them the means and opportunity. It was no wonder they had murder in mind for their relational databases. As the 2000s drew on, both companies produced brief but highly influential papers about their efforts: BigTable from Google and Dynamo from Amazon.

It's often said that Amazon and Google operate at scales far removed from most organizations, so the solutions they needed may not be relevant to an average organization. While it's true that most software projects don't need that level of scale, it's also true that more and more organizations are beginning to explore what they can do by capturing and processing more data—and to run into the same problems. So, as more information leaked out about what Google and Amazon had done, people began to explore making databases along similar lines—explicitly designed to live in a world of clusters. While the earlier menaces to relational dominance turned out to be phantoms, the threat from clusters was serious.

1.5 The Emergence of NoSQL

It's a wonderful irony that the term "NoSQL" first made its appearance in the late 90s as the name of an open-source relational database [Strozzi NoSQL]. Led by Carlo Strozzi, this database stores its tables as ASCII files, each tuple represented by a line with fields separated by tabs. The name comes from the fact that the database doesn't use SQL as a query language. Instead, the database is manipulated through shell scripts that can be combined into the usual UNIX pipelines. Other than the terminological coincidence, Strozzi's NoSQL had no influence on the databases we describe in this book.

The usage of "NoSQL" that we recognize today traces back to a meetup on June 11, 2009 in San Francisco organized by Johan Oskarsson, a software developer based in London. The example of BigTable and Dynamo had inspired a bunch of projects experimenting with alternative data storage, and discussions of these had become a feature of the better software conferences around that time. Johan was interested in finding out more about some of these new databases while he was in San Francisco for a Hadoop summit. Since he had little time there, he felt that it wouldn't be feasible to visit them all, so he decided to host a meetup where they could all come together and present their work to whoever was interested.

Johan wanted a name for the meetup—something that would make a good Twitter hashtag: short, memorable, and without too many Google hits so that a search on the name would quickly find the meetup. He asked for suggestions on the #cassandra IRC channel and got a few, selecting the suggestion of "NoSQL" from Eric Evans (a developer at Rackspace, no connection to the DDD Eric

Evans). While it had the disadvantage of being negative and not really describing these systems, it did fit the hashtag criteria. At the time they were thinking of only naming a single meeting and were not expecting it to catch on to name this entire technology trend [Oskarsson].

The term "NoSQL" caught on like wildfire, but it's never been a term that's had much in the way of a strong definition. The original call [NoSQL Meetup] for the meetup asked for "open-source, distributed, nonrelational databases." The talks there [NoSQL Debrief] were from Voldemort, Cassandra, Dynomite, HBase, Hypertable, CouchDB, and MongoDB—but the term has never been confined to that original septet. There's no generally accepted definition, nor an authority to provide one, so all we can do is discuss some common characteristics of the databases that tend to be called "NoSQL."

To begin with, there is the obvious point that NoSQL databases don't use SQL. Some of them do have query languages, and it makes sense for them to be similar to SQL in order to make them easier to learn. Cassandra's CQL is like this—"exactly like SQL (except where it's not)" [CQL]. But so far none have implemented anything that would fit even the rather flexible notion of standard SQL. It will be interesting to see what happens if an established NoSQL database decides to implement a reasonably standard SQL; the only predictable outcome for such an eventuality is plenty of argument.

Another important characteristic of these databases is that they are generally open-source projects. Although the term NoSQL is frequently applied to closed-source systems, there's a notion that NoSQL is an open-source phenomenon.

Most NoSQL databases are driven by the need to run on clusters, and this is certainly true of those that were talked about during the initial meetup. This has an effect on their data model as well as their approach to consistency. Relational databases use ACID transactions (p. 19) to handle consistency across the whole database. This inherently clashes with a cluster environment, so NoSQL databases offer a range of options for consistency and distribution.

However, not all NoSQL databases are strongly oriented towards running on clusters. Graph databases are one style of NoSQL databases that uses a distribution model similar to relational databases but offers a different data model that makes it better at handling data with complex relationships.

NoSQL databases are generally based on the needs of the early 21st century web estates, so usually only systems developed during that time frame are called NoSQL—thus ruling out hoards of databases created before the new millennium, let alone BC (Before Codd).

NoSQL databases operate without a schema, allowing you to freely add fields to database records without having to define any changes in structure first. This is particularly useful when dealing with nonuniform data and custom fields which forced relational databases to use names like `customField6` or custom field tables that are awkward to process and understand.

All of the above are common characteristics of things that we see described as NoSQL databases. None of these are definitional, and indeed it's likely that there will never be a coherent definition of "NoSQL" (sigh). However, this crude set of characteristics has been our guide in writing this book. Our chief enthusiasm with this subject is that the rise of NoSQL has opened up the range of options for data storage. Consequently, this opening up shouldn't be confined to what's usually classed as a NoSQL store. We hope that other data storage options will become more acceptable, including many that predate the NoSQL movement. There is a limit, however, to what we can usefully discuss in this book, so we've decided to concentrate on this noDefinition.

When you first hear "NoSQL," an immediate question is what does it stand for—a "no" to SQL? Most people who talk about NoSQL say that it really means "Not Only SQL," but this interpretation has a couple of problems. Most people write "NoSQL" whereas "Not Only SQL" would be written "NOSQL." Also, there wouldn't be much point in calling something a NoSQL database under the "not only" meaning—because then, Oracle or Postgres would fit that definition, we would prove that black equals white and would all get run over on crosswalks.

To resolve this, we suggest that you don't worry about what the term stands for, but rather about what it means (which is recommended with most acronyms). Thus, when "NoSQL" is applied to a database, it refers to an ill-defined set of mostly open-source databases, mostly developed in the early 21st century, and mostly not using SQL.

The "not-only" interpretation does have its value, as it describes the ecosystem that many people think is the future of databases. This is in fact what we consider to be the most important contribution of this way of thinking—it's better to think of NoSQL as a movement rather than a technology. We don't think that relational databases are going away—they are still going to be the most common form of database in use. Even though we've written this book, we still recommend relational databases. Their familiarity, stability, feature set, and available support are compelling arguments for most projects.

The change is that now we see relational databases as one option for data storage. This point of view is often referred to as **polyglot persistence**—using different data stores in different circumstances. Instead of just picking a relational database because everyone does, we need to understand the nature of the data we're storing and how we want to manipulate it. The result is that most organizations will have a mix of data storage technologies for different circumstances.

In order to make this polyglot world work, our view is that organizations also need to shift from integration databases to application databases. Indeed, we assume in this book that you'll be using a NoSQL database as an application database; we don't generally consider NoSQL databases a good choice for integration databases. We don't see this as a disadvantage as we think that even if you don't use NoSQL, shifting to encapsulating data in services is a good direction to take.

In our account of the history of NoSQL development, we've concentrated on big data running on clusters. While we think this is the key thing that drove the opening up of the database world, it isn't the only reason we see project teams considering NoSQL databases. An equally important reason is the old frustration with the impedance mismatch problem. The big data concerns have created an opportunity for people to think freshly about their data storage needs, and some development teams see that using a NoSQL database can help their productivity by simplifying their database access even if they have no need to scale beyond a single machine.

So, as you read the rest of this book, remember there are two primary reasons for considering NoSQL. One is to handle data access with sizes and performance that demand a cluster; the other is to improve the productivity of application development by using a more convenient data interaction style.

1.6 Key Points

- Relational databases have been a successful technology for twenty years, providing persistence, concurrency control, and an integration mechanism.

- Application developers have been frustrated with the impedance mismatch between the relational model and the in-memory data structures.

- There is a movement away from using databases as integration points towards encapsulating databases within applications and integrating through services.

- The vital factor for a change in data storage was the need to support large volumes of data by running on clusters. Relational databases are not designed to run efficiently on clusters.

- NoSQL is an accidental neologism. There is no prescriptive definition—all you can make is an observation of common characteristics.

- The common characteristics of NoSQL databases are

  - Not using the relational model

  - Running well on clusters

  - Open-source

  - Built for the 21st century web estates

  - Schemaless

- The most important result of the rise of NoSQL is Polyglot Persistence.

Chapter 2

Aggregate Data Models

A data model is the model through which we perceive and manipulate our data. For people using a database, the data model describes how we interact with the data in the database. This is distinct from a storage model, which describes how the database stores and manipulates the data internally. In an ideal world, we should be ignorant of the storage model, but in practice we need at least some inkling of it—primarily to achieve decent performance.

In conversation, the term "data model" often means the model of the specific data in an application. A developer might point to an entity-relationship diagram of their database and refer to that as their data model containing customers, orders, products, and the like. However, in this book we'll mostly be using "data model" to refer to the model by which the database organizes data—what might be more formally called a metamodel.

The dominant data model of the last couple of decades is the relational data model, which is best visualized as a set of tables, rather like a page of a spreadsheet. Each table has rows, with each row representing some entity of interest. We describe this entity through columns, each having a single value. A column may refer to another row in the same or different table, which constitutes a relationship between those entities. (We're using informal but common terminology when we speak of tables and rows; the more formal terms would be relations and tuples.)

One of the most obvious shifts with NoSQL is a move away from the relational model. Each NoSQL solution has a different model that it uses, which we put into four categories widely used in the NoSQL ecosystem: key-value, document, column-family, and graph. Of these, the first three share a common characteristic of their data models which we will call aggregate orientation. In this chapter we'll explain what we mean by aggregate orientation and what it means for data models.

2.1 Aggregates

The relational model takes the information that we want to store and divides it into tuples (rows). A tuple is a limited data structure: It captures a set of values, so you cannot nest one tuple within another to get nested records, nor can you put a list of values or tuples within another. This simplicity underpins the relational model—it allows us to think of all operations as operating on and returning tuples.

Aggregate orientation takes a different approach. It recognizes that often, you want to operate on data in units that have a more complex structure than a set of tuples. It can be handy to think in terms of a complex record that allows lists and other record structures to be nested inside it. As we'll see, key-value, document, and column-family databases all make use of this more complex record. However, there is no common term for this complex record; in this book we use the term "aggregate."

Aggregate is a term that comes from Domain-Driven Design [Evans]. In Domain-Driven Design, an **aggregate** is a collection of related objects that we wish to treat as a unit. In particular, it is a unit for data manipulation and management of consistency. Typically, we like to update aggregates with atomic operations and communicate with our data storage in terms of aggregates. This definition matches really well with how key-value, document, and column-family databases work. Dealing in aggregates makes it much easier for these databases to handle operating on a cluster, since the aggregate makes a natural unit for replication and sharding. Aggregates are also often easier for application programmers to work with, since they often manipulate data through aggregate structures.

2.1.1 Example of Relations and Aggregates

At this point, an example may help explain what we're talking about. Let's assume we have to build an e-commerce website; we are going to be selling items directly to customers over the web, and we will have to store information about users, our product catalog, orders, shipping addresses, billing addresses, and payment data. We can use this scenario to model the data using a relation data store as well as NoSQL data stores and talk about their pros and cons. For a relational database, we might start with a data model shown in Figure 2.1.

Figure 2.2 presents some sample data for this model.

As we're good relational soldiers, everything is properly normalized, so that no data is repeated in multiple tables. We also have referential integrity. A realistic order system would naturally be more involved than this, but this is the benefit of the rarefied air of a book.

Now let's see how this model might look when we think in more aggregate-oriented terms (Figure 2.3).

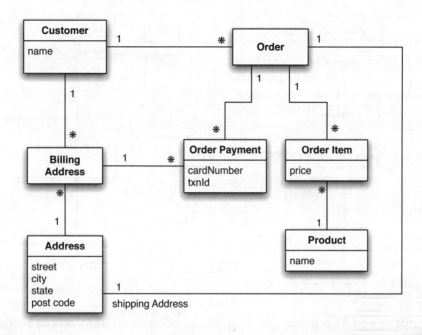

Figure 2.1 *Data model oriented around a relational database (using UML notation [Fowler UML])*

Customer

Id	Name
1	Martin

Order

Id	CustomerId	ShippingAddressId
99	1	77

Product

Id	Name
27	NoSQL Distilled

BillingAddress

Id	CustomerId	AddressId
55	1	77

OrderItem

Id	OrderId	ProductId	Price
100	99	27	32.45

Address

Id	City
77	Chicago

OrderPayment

Id	OrderId	CardNumber	BillingAddressId	txnId
33	99	1000-1000	55	abelif879rft

Figure 2.2 *Typical data using RDBMS data model*

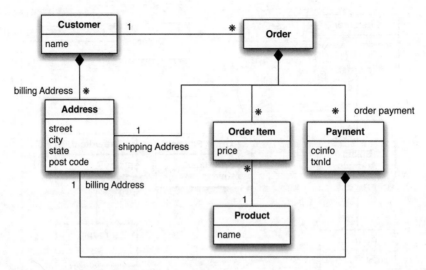

Figure 2.3 *An aggregate data model*

Again, we have some sample data, which we'll show in JSON format as that's a common representation for data in NoSQL land.

```
// in customers
{
"id":1,
"name":"Martin",
"billingAddress":[{"city":"Chicago"}]
}

// in orders
{
"id":99,
"customerId":1,
"orderItems":[
   {
   "productId":27,
   "price": 32.45,
   "productName": "NoSQL Distilled"
   }
   ],
"shippingAddress":[{"city":"Chicago"}]
"orderPayment":[
   {
      "ccinfo":"1000-1000-1000-1000",
      "txnId":"abelif879rft",
      "billingAddress": {"city": "Chicago"}
   }
   ],
}
```

In this model, we have two main aggregates: customer and order. We've used the black-diamond composition marker in UML to show how data fits into the aggregation structure. The customer contains a list of billing addresses; the order contains a list of order items, a shipping address, and payments. The payment itself contains a billing address for that payment.

A single logical address record appears three times in the example data, but instead of using IDs it's treated as a value and copied each time. This fits the domain where we would not want the shipping address, nor the payment's billing address, to change. In a relational database, we would ensure that the address rows aren't updated for this case, making a new row instead. With aggregates, we can copy the whole address structure into the aggregate as we need to.

The link between the customer and the order isn't within either aggregate—it's a relationship between aggregates. Similarly, the link from an order item would cross into a separate aggregate structure for products, which we haven't gone into. We've shown the product name as part of the order item here—this kind of denormalization is similar to the tradeoffs with relational databases, but is more common with aggregates because we want to minimize the number of aggregates we access during a data interaction.

The important thing to notice here isn't the particular way we've drawn the aggregate boundary so much as the fact that you have to think about accessing that data—and make that part of your thinking when developing the application data model. Indeed we could draw our aggregate boundaries differently, putting all the orders for a customer into the customer aggregate (Figure 2.4).

Using the above data model, an example `Customer` and `Order` would look like this:

```
// in customers
{
"customer": {
"id": 1,
"name": "Martin",
"billingAddress": [{"city": "Chicago"}],
"orders": [
  {
    "id":99,
    "customerId":1,
    "orderItems":[
    {
    "productId":27,
    "price": 32.45,
    "productName": "NoSQL Distilled"
    }
  ],
  "shippingAddress":[{"city":"Chicago"}]
```

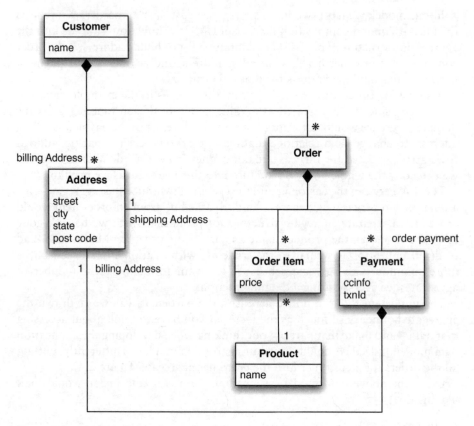

Figure 2.4 *Embed all the objects for customer and the customer's orders*

```
"orderPayment":[
  {
  "ccinfo":"1000-1000-1000-1000",
  "txnId":"abelif879rft",
  "billingAddress": {"city": "Chicago"}
  }],
 }]
}
}
```

Like most things in modeling, there's no universal answer for how to draw your aggregate boundaries. It depends entirely on how you tend to manipulate your data. If you tend to access a customer together with all of that customer's orders at once, then you would prefer a single aggregate. However, if you tend to focus on accessing a single order at a time, then you should prefer having separate aggregates for each order. Naturally, this is very context-specific; some applications will prefer one or the other, even within a single system, which is exactly why many people prefer aggregate ignorance.

2.1.2 Consequences of Aggregate Orientation

While the relational mapping captures the various data elements and their relationships reasonably well, it does so without any notion of an aggregate entity. In our domain language, we might say that an order consists of order items, a shipping address, and a payment. This can be expressed in the relational model in terms of foreign key relationships—but there is nothing to distinguish relationships that represent aggregations from those that don't. As a result, the database can't use a knowledge of aggregate structure to help it store and distribute the data.

Various data modeling techniques have provided ways of marking aggregate or composite structures. The problem, however, is that modelers rarely provide any semantics for what makes an aggregate relationship different from any other; where there are semantics, they vary. When working with aggregate-oriented databases, we have a clearer semantics to consider by focusing on the unit of interaction with the data storage. It is, however, not a logical data property: It's all about how the data is being used by applications—a concern that is often outside the bounds of data modeling.

Relational databases have no concept of aggregate within their data model, so we call them **aggregate-ignorant**. In the NoSQL world, graph databases are also aggregate-ignorant. Being aggregate-ignorant is not a bad thing. It's often difficult to draw aggregate boundaries well, particularly if the same data is used in many different contexts. An order makes a good aggregate when a customer is making and reviewing orders, and when the retailer is processing orders. However, if a retailer wants to analyze its product sales over the last few months, then an order aggregate becomes a trouble. To get to product sales history, you'll have to dig into every aggregate in the database. So an aggregate structure may help with some data interactions but be an obstacle for others. An aggregate-ignorant model allows you to easily look at the data in different ways, so it is a better choice when you don't have a primary structure for manipulating your data.

The clinching reason for aggregate orientation is that it helps greatly with running on a cluster, which as you'll remember is the killer argument for the rise of NoSQL. If we're running on a cluster, we need to minimize how many nodes we need to query when we are gathering data. By explicitly including aggregates, we give the database important information about which bits of data will be manipulated together, and thus should live on the same node.

Aggregates have an important consequence for transactions. Relational databases allow you to manipulate any combination of rows from any tables in a single transaction. Such transactions are called **ACID transactions**: Atomic, Consistent, Isolated, and Durable. ACID is a rather contrived acronym; the real point is the atomicity: Many rows spanning many tables are updated as a single operation. This operation either succeeds or fails in its entirety, and concurrent operations are isolated from each other so they cannot see a partial update.

It's often said that NoSQL databases don't support ACID transactions and thus sacrifice consistency. This is a rather sweeping simplification. In general, it's true that aggregate-oriented databases don't have ACID transactions that span multiple aggregates. Instead, they support atomic manipulation of a single aggregate at a time. This means that if we need to manipulate multiple aggregates in an atomic way, we have to manage that ourselves in the application code. In practice, we find that most of the time we are able to keep our atomicity needs to within a single aggregate; indeed, that's part of the consideration for deciding how to divide up our data into aggregates. We should also remember that graph and other aggregate-ignorant databases usually do support ACID transactions similar to relational databases. Above all, the topic of consistency is much more involved than whether a database is ACID or not, as we'll explore in Chapter 5.

2.2 Key-Value and Document Data Models

We said earlier on that key-value and document databases were strongly aggregate-oriented. What we meant by this was that we think of these databases as primarily constructed through aggregates. Both of these types of databases consist of lots of aggregates with each aggregate having a key or ID that's used to get at the data.

The two models differ in that in a key-value database, the aggregate is opaque to the database—just some big blob of mostly meaningless bits. In contrast, a document database is able to see a structure in the aggregate. The advantage of opacity is that we can store whatever we like in the aggregate. The database may impose some general size limit, but other than that we have complete freedom. A document database imposes limits on what we can place in it, defining allowable structures and types. In return, however, we get more flexibility in access.

With a key-value store, we can only access an aggregate by lookup based on its key. With a document database, we can submit queries to the database based on the fields in the aggregate, we can retrieve part of the aggregate rather than the whole thing, and the database can create indexes based on the contents of the aggregate.

In practice, the line between key-value and document gets a bit blurry. People often put an ID field in a document database to do a key-value style lookup. Databases classified as key-value databases may allow you structures for data beyond just an opaque aggregate. For example, Riak allows you to add metadata to aggregates for indexing and interaggregate links, Redis allows you to break down the aggregate into lists or sets. You can support querying by integrating search tools such as Solr. As an example, Riak includes a search facility that uses Solr-like searching on any aggregates that are stored as JSON or XML structures.

Despite this blurriness, the general distinction still holds. With key-value databases, we expect to mostly look up aggregates using a key. With document databases, we mostly expect to submit some form of query based on the internal structure of the document; this might be a key, but it's more likely to be something else.

2.3 Column-Family Stores

One of the early and influential NoSQL databases was Google's BigTable [Chang etc.]. Its name conjured up a tabular structure which it realized with sparse columns and no schema. As you'll soon see, it doesn't help to think of this structure as a table; rather, it is a two-level map. But, however you think about the structure, it has been a model that influenced later databases such as HBase and Cassandra.

These databases with a bigtable-style data model are often referred to as column stores, but that name has been around for a while to describe a different animal. Pre-NoSQL column stores, such as C-Store [C-Store], were happy with SQL and the relational model. The thing that made them different was the way in which they physically stored data. Most databases have a row as a unit of storage which, in particular, helps write performance. However, there are many scenarios where writes are rare, but you often need to read a few columns of many rows at once. In this situation, it's better to store groups of columns for all rows as the basic storage unit—which is why these databases are called column stores.

Bigtable and its offspring follow this notion of storing groups of columns (column families) together, but part company with C-Store and friends by abandoning the relational model and SQL. In this book, we refer to this class of databases as column-family databases.

Perhaps the best way to think of the column-family model is as a two-level aggregate structure. As with key-value stores, the first key is often described as a row identifier, picking up the aggregate of interest. The difference with column-family structures is that this row aggregate is itself formed of a map of more detailed values. These second-level values are referred to as columns. As well as accessing the row as a whole, operations also allow picking out a particular column, so to get a particular customer's name from Figure 2.5 you could do something like get('1234', 'name').

Column-family databases organize their columns into column families. Each column has to be part of a single column family, and the column acts as unit for access, with the assumption that data for a particular column family will be usually accessed together.

This also gives you a couple of ways to think about how the data is structured.

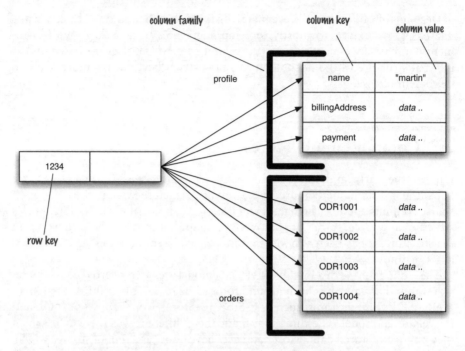

Figure 2.5 *Representing customer information in a column-family structure*

- Row-oriented: Each row is an aggregate (for example, customer with the ID of 1234) with column families representing useful chunks of data (profile, order history) within that aggregate.

- Column-oriented: Each column family defines a record type (e.g., customer profiles) with rows for each of the records. You then think of a row as the join of records in all column families.

This latter aspect reflects the columnar nature of column-family databases. Since the database knows about these common groupings of data, it can use this information for its storage and access behavior. Even though a document database declares some structure to the database, each document is still seen as a single unit. Column families give a two-dimensional quality to column-family databases.

This terminology is as established by Google Bigtable and HBase, but Cassandra looks at things slightly differently. A row in Cassandra only occurs in one column family, but that column family may contain supercolumns—columns that contain nested columns. The supercolumns in Cassandra are the best equivalent to the classic Bigtable column families.

It can still be confusing to think of column-families as tables. You can add any column to any row, and rows can have very different column keys. While new columns are added to rows during regular database access, defining new column families is much rarer and may involve stopping the database for it to happen.

The example of Figure 2.5 illustrates another aspect of column-family databases that may be unfamiliar for people used to relational tables: the `orders` column family. Since columns can be added freely, you can model a list of items by making each item a separate column. This is very odd if you think of a column family as a table, but quite natural if you think of a column-family row as an aggregate. Cassandra uses the terms "wide" and "skinny." **Skinny rows** have few columns with the same columns used across the many different rows. In this case, the column family defines a record type, each row is a record, and each column is a field. A **wide row** has many columns (perhaps thousands), with rows having very different columns. A wide column family models a list, with each column being one element in that list.

A consequence of wide column families is that a column family may define a sort order for its columns. This way we can access orders by their order key and access ranges of orders by their keys. While this might not be useful if we keyed orders by their IDs, it would be if we made the key out of a concatenation of date and ID (e.g., `20111027-1001`).

Although it's useful to distinguish column families by their wide or skinny nature, there's no technical reason why a column family cannot contain both field-like columns and list-like columns—although doing this would confuse the sort ordering.

2.4 Summarizing Aggregate-Oriented Databases

At this point, we've covered enough material to give you a reasonable overview of the three different styles of aggregate-oriented data models and how they differ.

What they all share is the notion of an aggregate indexed by a key that you can use for lookup. This aggregate is central to running on a cluster, as the database will ensure that all the data for an aggregate is stored together on one node. The aggregate also acts as the atomic unit for updates, providing a useful, if limited, amount of transactional control.

Within that notion of aggregate, we have some differences. The key-value data model treats the aggregate as an opaque whole, which means you can only do key lookup for the whole aggregate—you cannot run a query nor retrieve a part of the aggregate.

The document model makes the aggregate transparent to the database allowing you to do queries and partial retrievals. However, since the document has no schema, the database cannot act much on the structure of the document to optimize the storage and retrieval of parts of the aggregate.

Column-family models divide the aggregate into column families, allowing the database to treat them as units of data within the row aggregate. This imposes some structure on the aggregate but allows the database to take advantage of that structure to improve its accessibility.

2.5 Further Reading

For more on the general concept of aggregates, which are often used with relational databases too, see [Evans]. The Domain-Driven Design community is the best source for further information about aggregates—recent information usually appears at http://domaindrivendesign.org.

2.6 Key Points

- An aggregate is a collection of data that we interact with as a unit. Aggregates form the boundaries for ACID operations with the database.

- Key-value, document, and column-family databases can all be seen as forms of aggregate-oriented database.

- Aggregates make it easier for the database to manage data storage over clusters.

- Aggregate-oriented databases work best when most data interaction is done with the same aggregate; aggregate-ignorant databases are better when interactions use data organized in many different formations.

Chapter 3

More Details on Data Models

So far we've covered the key feature in most NoSQL databases: their use of aggregates and how aggregate-oriented databases model aggregates in different ways. While aggregates are a central part of the NoSQL story, there is more to the data modeling side than that, and we'll explore these further concepts in this chapter.

3.1 Relationships

Aggregates are useful in that they put together data that is commonly accessed together. But there are still lots of cases where data that's related is accessed differently. Consider the relationship between a customer and all of his orders. Some applications will want to access the order history whenever they access the customer; this fits in well with combining the customer with his order history into a single aggregate. Other applications, however, want to process orders individually and thus model orders as independent aggregates.

In this case, you'll want separate order and customer aggregates but with some kind of relationship between them so that any work on an order can look up customer data. The simplest way to provide such a link is to embed the ID of the customer within the order's aggregate data. That way, if you need data from the customer record, you read the order, ferret out the customer ID, and make another call to the database to read the customer data. This will work, and will be just fine in many scenarios—but the database will be ignorant of the relationship in the data. This can be important because there are times when it's useful for the database to know about these links.

As a result, many databases—even key-value stores—provide ways to make these relationships visible to the database. Document stores make the content of the aggregate available to the database to form indexes and queries. Riak, a key-value store, allows you to put link information in metadata, supporting partial retrieval and link-walking capability.

25

An important aspect of relationships between aggregates is how they handle updates. Aggregate-oriented databases treat the aggregate as the unit of data-retrieval. Consequently, atomicity is only supported within the contents of a single aggregate. If you update multiple aggregates at once, you have to deal yourself with a failure partway through. Relational databases help you with this by allowing you to modify multiple records in a single transaction, providing ACID guarantees while altering many rows.

All of this means that aggregate-oriented databases become more awkward as you need to operate across multiple aggregates. There are various ways to deal with this, which we'll explore later in this chapter, but the fundamental awkwardness remains.

This may imply that if you have data based on lots of relationships, you should prefer a relational database over a NoSQL store. While that's true for aggregate-oriented databases, it's worth remembering that relational databases aren't all that stellar with complex relationships either. While you can express queries involving joins in SQL, things quickly get very hairy—both with SQL writing and with the resulting performance—as the number of joins mounts up.

This makes it a good moment to introduce another category of databases that's often lumped into the NoSQL pile.

3.2 Graph Databases

Graph databases are an odd fish in the NoSQL pond. Most NoSQL databases were inspired by the need to run on clusters, which led to aggregate-oriented data models of large records with simple connections. Graph databases are motivated by a different frustration with relational databases and thus have an opposite model—small records with complex interconnections, something like Figure 3.1.

In this context, a graph isn't a bar chart or histogram; instead, we refer to a graph data structure of nodes connected by edges.

In Figure 3.1 we have a web of information whose nodes are very small (nothing more than a name) but there is a rich structure of interconnections between them. With this structure, we can ask questions such as "find the books in the Databases category that are written by someone whom a friend of mine likes."

Graph databases specialize in capturing this sort of information—but on a much larger scale than a readable diagram could capture. This is ideal for capturing any data consisting of complex relationships such as social networks, product preferences, or eligibility rules.

The fundamental data model of a graph database is very simple: nodes connected by edges (also called arcs). Beyond this essential characteristic there is a lot of variation in data models—in particular, what mechanisms you have

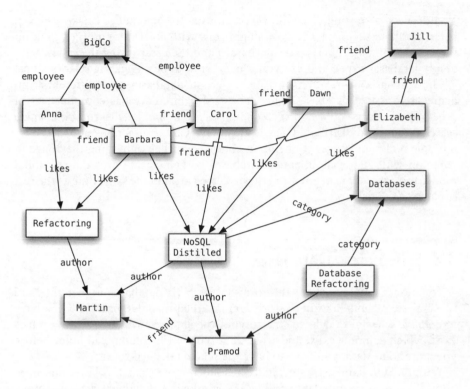

Figure 3.1 *An example graph structure*

to store data in your nodes and edges. A quick sample of some current capabilities illustrates this variety of possibilities: FlockDB is simply nodes and edges with no mechanism for additional attributes; Neo4J allows you to attach Java objects as properties to nodes and edges in a schemaless fashion ("Features," p. 113); Infinite Graph stores your Java objects, which are subclasses of its built-in types, as nodes and edges.

Once you have built up a graph of nodes and edges, a graph database allows you to query that network with query operations designed with this kind of graph in mind. This is where the important differences between graph and relational databases come in. Although relational databases can implement relationships using foreign keys, the joins required to navigate around can get quite expensive—which means performance is often poor for highly connected data models. Graph databases make traversal along the relationships very cheap. A large part of this is because graph databases shift most of the work of navigating relationships from query time to insert time. This naturally pays off for situations where querying performance is more important than insert speed.

Most of the time you find data by navigating through the network of edges, with queries such as "tell me all the things that both Anna and Barbara like."

You do need a starting place, however, so usually some nodes can be indexed by an attribute such as ID. So you might start with an ID lookup (i.e., look up the people named "Anna" and "Barbara") and then start using the edges. Still, graph databases expect most of your query work to be navigating relationships.

The emphasis on relationships makes graph databases very different from aggregate-oriented databases. This data model difference has consequences in other aspects, too; you'll find such databases are more likely to run on a single server rather than distributed across clusters. ACID transactions need to cover multiple nodes and edges to maintain consistency. The only thing they have in common with aggregate-oriented databases is their rejection of the relational model and an upsurge in attention they received around the same time as the rest of the NoSQL field.

3.3 Schemaless Databases

A common theme across all the forms of NoSQL databases is that they are schemaless. When you want to store data in a relational database, you first have to define a schema—a defined structure for the database which says what tables exist, which columns exist, and what data types each column can hold. Before you store some data, you have to have the schema defined for it.

With NoSQL databases, storing data is much more casual. A key-value store allows you to store any data you like under a key. A document database effectively does the same thing, since it makes no restrictions on the structure of the documents you store. Column-family databases allow you to store any data under any column you like. Graph databases allow you to freely add new edges and freely add properties to nodes and edges as you wish.

Advocates of schemalessness rejoice in this freedom and flexibility. With a schema, you have to figure out in advance what you need to store, but that can be hard to do. Without a schema binding you, you can easily store whatever you need. This allows you to easily change your data storage as you learn more about your project. You can easily add new things as you discover them. Furthermore, if you find you don't need some things anymore, you can just stop storing them, without worrying about losing old data as you would if you delete columns in a relational schema.

As well as handling changes, a schemaless store also makes it easier to deal with **nonuniform data**: data where each record has a different set of fields. A schema puts all rows of a table into a straightjacket, which becomes awkward if you have different kinds of data in different rows. You either end up with lots of columns that are usually null (a sparse table), or you end up with meaningless columns like `custom column 4`. Schemalessness avoids this, allowing each record to contain just what it needs—no more, no less.

Schemalessness is appealing, and it certainly avoids many problems that exist with fixed-schema databases, but it brings some problems of its own. If all you are doing is storing some data and displaying it in a report as a simple list of fieldName: value lines then a schema is only going to get in the way. But usually we do with our data more than this, and we do it with programs that need to know that the billing address is called billingAddress and not addressForBilling and that the quantify field is going to be an integer 5 and not five.

The vital, if sometimes inconvenient, fact is that whenever we write a program that accesses data, that program almost always relies on some form of implicit schema. Unless it just says something like

```
//pseudo code
foreach (Record r in records) {
  foreach (Field f in r.fields) {
    print (f.name, f.value)
  }
}
```

it will assume that certain field names are present and carry data with a certain meaning, and assume something about the type of data stored within that field. Programs are not humans; they cannot read "qty" and infer that that must be the same as "quantity"—at least not unless we specifically program them to do so. So, however schemaless our database is, there is usually an implicit schema present. This **implicit schema** is a set of assumptions about the data's structure in the code that manipulates the data.

Having the implicit schema in the application code results in some problems. It means that in order to understand what data is present you have to dig into the application code. If that code is well structured you should be able to find a clear place from which to deduce the schema. But there are no guarantees; it all depends on how clear the application code is. Furthermore, the database remains ignorant of the schema—it can't use the schema to help it decide how to store and retrieve data efficiently. It can't apply its own validations upon that data to ensure that different applications don't manipulate data in an inconsistent way.

These are the reasons why relational databases have a fixed schema, and indeed the reasons why most databases have had fixed schemas in the past. Schemas have value, and the rejection of schemas by NoSQL databases is indeed quite startling.

Essentially, a schemaless database shifts the schema into the application code that accesses it. This becomes problematic if multiple applications, developed by different people, access the same database. These problems can be reduced with a couple of approaches. One is to encapsulate all database interaction within a single application and integrate it with other applications using web services. This fits in well with many people's current preference for using web services for integration. Another approach is to clearly delineate different areas of an aggregate for access by different applications. These could be different sections in a document database or different column families in a column-family database.

Although NoSQL fans often criticize relational schemas for having to be defined up front and being inflexible, that's not really true. Relational schemas can be changed at any time with standard SQL commands. If necessary, you can create new columns in an ad-hoc way to store nonuniform data. We have only rarely seen this done, but it worked reasonably well where we have. Most of the time, however, nonuniformity in your data is a good reason to favor a schemaless database.

Schemalessness does have a big impact on changes of a database's structure over time, particularly for more uniform data. Although it's not practiced as widely as it ought to be, changing a relational database's schema can be done in a controlled way. Similarly, you have to exercise control when changing how you store data in a schemaless database so that you can easily access both old and new data. Furthermore, the flexibility that schemalessness gives you only applies within an aggregate—if you need to change your aggregate boundaries, the migration is every bit as complex as it is in the relational case. We'll talk more about database migration later ("Schema Migrations," p. 123).

3.4 Materialized Views

When we talked about aggregate-oriented data models, we stressed their advantages. If you want to access orders, it's useful to have all the data for an order contained in a single aggregate that can be stored and accessed as a unit. But aggregate-orientation has a corresponding disadvantage: What happens if a product manager wants to know how much a particular item has sold over the last couple of weeks? Now the aggregate-orientation works against you, forcing you to potentially read every order in the database to answer the question. You can reduce this burden by building an index on the product, but you're still working against the aggregate structure.

Relational databases have an advantage here because their lack of aggregate structure allows them to support accessing data in different ways. Furthermore, they provide a convenient mechanism that allows you to look at data differently from the way it's stored—views. A view is like a relational table (it is a relation) but it's defined by computation over the base tables. When you access a view, the database computes the data in the view—a handy form of encapsulation.

Views provide a mechanism to hide from the client whether data is derived data or base data—but can't avoid the fact that some views are expensive to compute. To cope with this, **materialized views** were invented, which are views that are computed in advance and cached on disk. Materialized views are effective for data that is read heavily but can stand being somewhat stale.

Although NoSQL databases don't have views, they may have precomputed and cached queries, and they reuse the term "materialized view" to describe them. It's also much more of a central aspect for aggregate-oriented databases than it is for relational systems, since most applications will have to deal with some queries that don't fit well with the aggregate structure. (Often, NoSQL databases create materialized views using a map-reduce computation, which we'll talk about in Chapter 7.)

There are two rough strategies to building a materialized view. The first is the eager approach where you update the materialized view at the same time you update the base data for it. In this case, adding an order would also update the purchase history aggregates for each product. This approach is good when you have more frequent reads of the materialized view than you have writes and you want the materialized views to be as fresh as possible. The application database (p. 7) approach is valuable here as it makes it easier to ensure that any updates to base data also update materialized views.

If you don't want to pay that overhead on each update, you can run batch jobs to update the materialized views at regular intervals. You'll need to understand your business requirements to assess how stale your materialized views can be.

You can build materialized views outside of the database by reading the data, computing the view, and saving it back to the database. More often databases will support building materialized views themselves. In this case, you provide the computation that needs to be done, and the database executes the computation when needed according to some parameters that you configure. This is particularly handy for eager updates of views with incremental map-reduce ("Incremental Map-Reduce," p. 76).

Materialized views can be used within the same aggregate. An order document might include an order summary element that provides summary information about the order so that a query for an order summary does not have to transfer the entire order document. Using different column families for materialized views is a common feature of column-family databases. An advantage of doing this is that it allows you to update the materialized view within the same atomic operation.

3.5 Modeling for Data Access

As mentioned earlier, when modeling data aggregates we need to consider how the data is going to be read as well as what are the side effects on data related to those aggregates.

Let's start with the model where all the data for the customer is embedded using a key-value store (see Figure 3.2).

In this scenario, the application can read the customer's information and all the related data by using the key. If the requirements are to read the orders or the

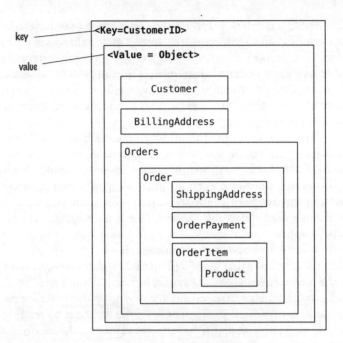

Figure 3.2 *Embed all the objects for customer and their orders.*

products sold in each order, the whole object has to be read and then parsed on the client side to build the results. When references are needed, we could switch to document stores and then query inside the documents, or even change the data for the key-value store to split the value object into `Customer` and `Order` objects and then maintain these objects' references to each other.

With the references (see Figure 3.3), we can now find the orders independently from the `Customer`, and with the `orderId` reference in the `Customer` we can find all `Orders` for the `Customer`. Using aggregates this way allows for read optimization, but we have to push the `orderId` reference into `Customer` every time with a new `Order`.

```
# Customer object
{
"customerId": 1,
"customer": {
  "name": "Martin",
  "billingAddress": [{"city": "Chicago"}],
  "payment": [{"type": "debit","ccinfo": "1000-1000-1000-1000"}],
  "orders":[{"orderId":99}]
  }
}
```

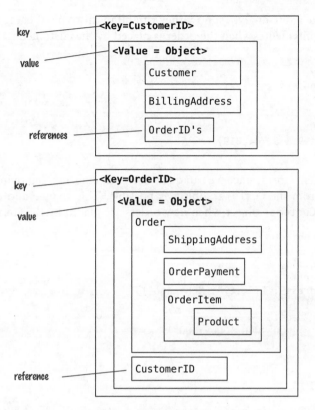

Figure 3.3 Customer *is stored separately from* Order.

```
# Order object
{
"customerId": 1,
"orderId": 99,
"order":{
  "orderDate":"Nov-20-2011",
  "orderItems":[{"productId":27, "price": 32.45}],
  "orderPayment":[{"ccinfo":"1000-1000-1000-1000",
          "txnId":"abelif879rft"}],
  "shippingAddress":{"city":"Chicago"}
  }
}
```

Aggregates can also be used to obtain analytics; for example, an aggregate update may fill in information on which Orders have a given Product in them. This denormalization of the data allows for fast access to the data we are interested in and is the basis for **Real Time BI** or **Real Time Analytics** where enterprises don't have to rely on end-of-the-day batch runs to populate data warehouse tables and generate analytics; now they can fill in this type of data, for multiple types of requirements, when the order is placed by the customer.

```
{
"itemid":27,
"orders":{99,545,897,678}
}
{
"itemid":29,
"orders":{199,545,704,819}
}
```

In document stores, since we can query inside documents, removing references to Orders from the Customer object is possible. This change allows us to not update the Customer object when new orders are placed by the Customer.

```
# Customer object
{
"customerId": 1,
"name": "Martin",
"billingAddress": [{"city": "Chicago"}],
"payment": [
  {"type": "debit",
  "ccinfo": "1000-1000-1000-1000"}
  ]
}
```

```
# Order object
{
"orderId": 99,
"customerId": 1,
"orderDate":"Nov-20-2011",
"orderItems":[{"productId":27, "price": 32.45}],
"orderPayment":[{"ccinfo":"1000-1000-1000-1000",
        "txnId":"abelif879rft"}],
"shippingAddress":{"city":"Chicago"}
}
```

Since document data stores allow you to query by attributes inside the document, searches such as "find all orders that include the *Refactoring Databases* product" are possible, but the decision to create an aggregate of items and orders they belong to is not based on the database's query capability but on the read optimization desired by the application.

When modeling for column-family stores, we have the benefit of the columns being ordered, allowing us to name columns that are frequently used so that they are fetched first. When using the column families to model the data, it is important to remember to do it per your query requirements and not for the purpose of writing; the general rule is to make it easy to query and denormalize the data during write.

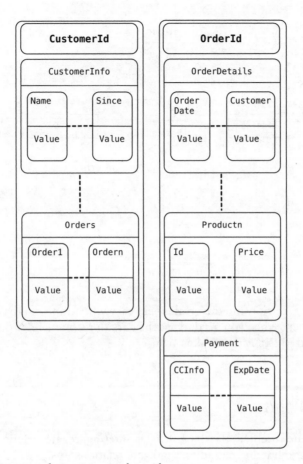

Figure 3.4 *Conceptual view into a column data store*

As you can imagine, there are multiple ways to model the data; one way is to store the Customer and Order in different *column-family* families (see Figure 3.4). Here, it is important to note the reference to all the orders placed by the customer are in the Customer column family. Similar other denormalizations are generally done so that query (read) performance is improved.

When using graph databases to model the same data, we model all objects as nodes and relations within them as relationships; these relationships have types and directional significance.

Each node has independent relationships with other nodes. These relationships have names like *PURCHASED, PAID_WITH*, or *BELONGS_TO* (see Figure 3.5); these relationship names let you traverse the graph. Let's say you want to find all the Customers who *PURCHASED* a product with the name *Refactoring Databases*. All we need to do is query for the product node Refactoring Databases and look for all the Customers with the incoming *PURCHASED* relationship.

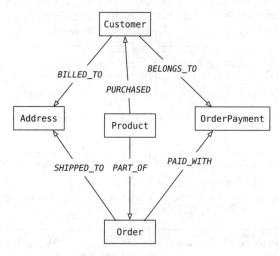

Figure 3.5   *Graph model of e-commerce data*

This type of relationship traversal is very easy with graph databases. It is especially convenient when you need to use the data to recommend products to users or to find patterns in actions taken by users.

3.6 Key Points

- Aggregate-oriented databases make inter-aggregate relationships more difficult to handle than intra-aggregate relationships.

- Graph databases organize data into node and edge graphs; they work best for data that has complex relationship structures.

- Schemaless databases allow you to freely add fields to records, but there is usually an implicit schema expected by users of the data.

- Aggregate-oriented databases often compute materialized views to provide data organized differently from their primary aggregates. This is often done with map-reduce computations.

Chapter 4

Distribution Models

The primary driver of interest in NoSQL has been its ability to run databases on a large cluster. As data volumes increase, it becomes more difficult and expensive to scale up—buy a bigger server to run the database on. A more appealing option is to scale out—run the database on a cluster of servers. Aggregate orientation fits well with scaling out because the aggregate is a natural unit to use for distribution.

Depending on your distribution model, you can get a data store that will give you the ability to handle larger quantities of data, the ability to process a greater read or write traffic, or more availability in the face of network slowdowns or breakages. These are often important benefits, but they come at a cost. Running over a cluster introduces complexity—so it's not something to do unless the benefits are compelling.

Broadly, there are two paths to data distribution: replication and sharding. Replication takes the same data and copies it over multiple nodes. Sharding puts different data on different nodes. Replication and sharding are orthogonal techniques: You can use either or both of them. Replication comes into two forms: master-slave and peer-to-peer. We will now discuss these techniques starting at the simplest and working up to the more complex: first single-server, then sharding, then master-slave replication, and finally peer-to-peer replication.

4.1 Single Server

The first and the simplest distribution option is the one we would most often recommend—no distribution at all. Run the database on a single machine that handles all the reads and writes to the data store. We prefer this option because it eliminates all the complexities that the other options introduce; it's easy for operations people to manage and easy for application developers to reason about.

Although a lot of NoSQL databases are designed around the idea of running on a cluster, it can make sense to use NoSQL with a single-server distribution model if the data model of the NoSQL store is more suited to the application. Graph databases are the obvious category here—these work best in a single-server configuration. If your data usage is mostly about processing aggregates, then a single-server document or key-value store may well be worthwhile because it's easier on application developers.

For the rest of this chapter we'll be wading through the advantages and complications of more sophisticated distribution schemes. Don't let the volume of words fool you into thinking that we would prefer these options. If we can get away without distributing our data, we will always choose a single-server approach.

4.2 Sharding

Often, a busy data store is busy because different people are accessing different parts of the dataset. In these circumstances we can support horizontal scalability by putting different parts of the data onto different servers—a technique that's called **sharding** (see Figure 4.1).

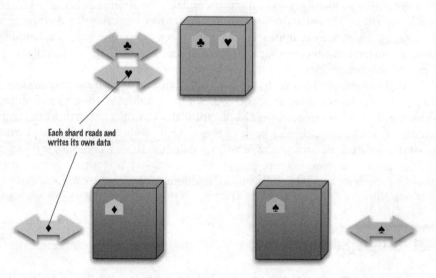

Each shard reads and writes its own data

Figure 4.1 *Sharding puts different data on separate nodes, each of which does its own reads and writes.*

In the ideal case, we have different users all talking to different server nodes. Each user only has to talk to one server, so gets rapid responses from that server.

The load is balanced out nicely between servers—for example, if we have ten servers, each one only has to handle 10% of the load.

Of course the ideal case is a pretty rare beast. In order to get close to it we have to ensure that data that's accessed together is clumped together on the same node and that these clumps are arranged on the nodes to provide the best data access.

The first part of this question is how to clump the data up so that one user mostly gets her data from a single server. This is where aggregate orientation comes in really handy. The whole point of aggregates is that we design them to combine data that's commonly accessed together—so aggregates leap out as an obvious unit of distribution.

When it comes to arranging the data on the nodes, there are several factors that can help improve performance. If you know that most accesses of certain aggregates are based on a physical location, you can place the data close to where it's being accessed. If you have orders for someone who lives in Boston, you can place that data in your eastern US data center.

Another factor is trying to keep the load even. This means that you should try to arrange aggregates so they are evenly distributed across the nodes which all get equal amounts of the load. This may vary over time, for example if some data tends to be accessed on certain days of the week—so there may be domain-specific rules you'd like to use.

In some cases, it's useful to put aggregates together if you think they may be read in sequence. The Bigtable paper [Chang etc.] described keeping its rows in lexicographic order and sorting web addresses based on reversed domain names (e.g., com.martinfowler). This way data for multiple pages could be accessed together to improve processing efficiency.

Historically most people have done sharding as part of application logic. You might put all customers with surnames starting from A to D on one shard and E to G on another. This complicates the programming model, as application code needs to ensure that queries are distributed across the various shards. Furthermore, rebalancing the sharding means changing the application code and migrating the data. Many NoSQL databases offer **auto-sharding**, where the database takes on the responsibility of allocating data to shards and ensuring that data access goes to the right shard. This can make it much easier to use sharding in an application.

Sharding is particularly valuable for performance because it can improve both read and write performance. Using replication, particularly with caching, can greatly improve read performance but does little for applications that have a lot of writes. Sharding provides a way to horizontally scale writes.

Sharding does little to improve resilience when used alone. Although the data is on different nodes, a node failure makes that shard's data unavailable just as surely as it does for a single-server solution. The resilience benefit it does provide is that only the users of the data on that shard will suffer; however, it's not good to have a database with part of its data missing. With a single server it's easier to pay the effort and cost to keep that server up and running; clusters usually try to use less reliable machines, and you're more likely to get a node failure. So in practice, sharding alone is likely to decrease resilience.

Despite the fact that sharding is made much easier with aggregates, it's still not a step to be taken lightly. Some databases are intended from the beginning to use sharding, in which case it's wise to run them on a cluster from the very beginning of development, and certainly in production. Other databases use sharding as a deliberate step up from a single-server configuration, in which case it's best to start single-server and only use sharding once your load projections clearly indicate that you are running out of headroom.

In any case the step from a single node to sharding is going to be tricky. We have heard tales of teams getting into trouble because they left sharding to very late, so when they turned it on in production their database became essentially unavailable because the sharding support consumed all the database resources for moving the data onto new shards. The lesson here is to use sharding well before you need to—when you have enough headroom to carry out the sharding.

4.3 Master-Slave Replication

With master-slave distribution, you replicate data across multiple nodes. One node is designated as the master, or primary. This master is the authoritative source for the data and is usually responsible for processing any updates to that data. The other nodes are slaves, or secondaries. A replication process synchronizes the slaves with the master (see Figure 4.2).

Master-slave replication is most helpful for scaling when you have a read-intensive dataset. You can scale horizontally to handle more read requests by adding more slave nodes and ensuring that all read requests are routed to the slaves. You are still, however, limited by the ability of the master to process updates and its ability to pass those updates on. Consequently it isn't such a good scheme for datasets with heavy write traffic, although offloading the read traffic will help a bit with handling the write load.

A second advantage of master-slave replication is **read resilience**: Should the master fail, the slaves can still handle read requests. Again, this is useful if most of your data access is reads. The failure of the master does eliminate the ability to handle writes until either the master is restored or a new master is appointed. However, having slaves as replicates of the master does speed up recovery after a failure of the master since a slave can be appointed a new master very quickly.

The ability to appoint a slave to replace a failed master means that master-slave replication is useful even if you don't need to scale out. All read and write traffic can go to the master while the slave acts as a hot backup. In this case it's

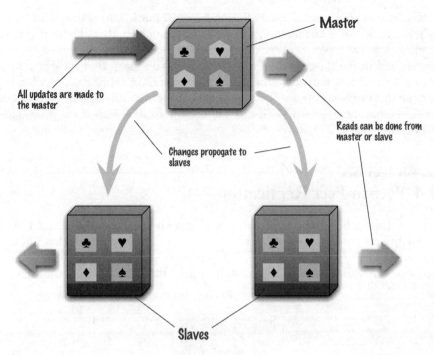

Figure 4.2 *Data is replicated from master to slaves. The master services all writes; reads may come from either master or slaves.*

easiest to think of the system as a single-server store with a hot backup. You get the convenience of the single-server configuration but with greater resilience—which is particularly handy if you want to be able to handle server failures gracefully.

Masters can be appointed manually or automatically. Manual appointing typically means that when you configure your cluster, you configure one node as the master. With automatic appointment, you create a cluster of nodes and they elect one of themselves to be the master. Apart from simpler configuration, automatic appointment means that the cluster can automatically appoint a new master when a master fails, reducing downtime.

In order to get read resilience, you need to ensure that the read and write paths into your application are different, so that you can handle a failure in the write path and still read. This includes such things as putting the reads and writes through separate database connections—a facility that is not often supported by database interaction libraries. As with any feature, you cannot be sure you have read resilience without good tests that disable the writes and check that reads still occur.

Replication comes with some alluring benefits, but it also comes with an inevitable dark side—inconsistency. You have the danger that different clients, reading different slaves, will see different values because the changes haven't all propagated to the slaves. In the worst case, that can mean that a client cannot read a write it just made. Even if you use master-slave replication just for hot backup this can be a concern, because if the master fails, any updates not passed on to the backup are lost. We'll talk about how to deal with these issues later ("Consistency," p. 47).

4.4 Peer-to-Peer Replication

Master-slave replication helps with read scalability but doesn't help with scalability of writes. It provides resilience against failure of a slave, but not of a master. Essentially, the master is still a bottleneck and a single point of failure. Peer-to-peer replication (see Figure 4.3) attacks these problems by not having

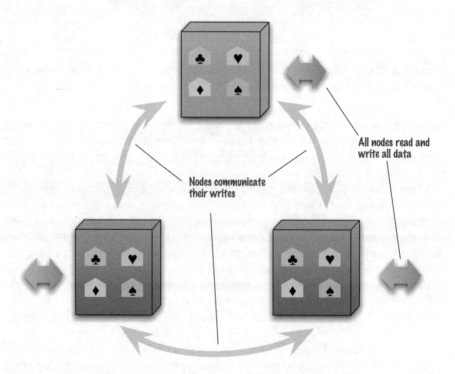

Figure 4.3 *Peer-to-peer replication has all nodes applying reads and writes to all the data.*

a master. All the replicas have equal weight, they can all accept writes, and the loss of any of them doesn't prevent access to the data store.

The prospect here looks mighty fine. With a peer-to-peer replication cluster, you can ride over node failures without losing access to data. Furthermore, you can easily add nodes to improve your performance. There's much to like here—but there are complications.

The biggest complication is, again, consistency. When you can write to two different places, you run the risk that two people will attempt to update the same record at the same time—a write-write conflict. Inconsistencies on read lead to problems but at least they are relatively transient. Inconsistent writes are forever.

We'll talk more about how to deal with write inconsistencies later on, but for the moment we'll note a couple of broad options. At one end, we can ensure that whenever we write data, the replicas coordinate to ensure we avoid a conflict. This can give us just as strong a guarantee as a master, albeit at the cost of network traffic to coordinate the writes. We don't need all the replicas to agree on the write, just a majority, so we can still survive losing a minority of the replica nodes.

At the other extreme, we can decide to cope with an inconsistent write. There are contexts when we can come up with policy to merge inconsistent writes. In this case we can get the full performance benefit of writing to any replica.

These points are at the ends of a spectrum where we trade off consistency for availability.

4.5 Combining Sharding and Replication

Replication and sharding are strategies that can be combined. If we use both master-slave replication and sharding (see Figure 4.4), this means that we have multiple masters, but each data item only has a single master. Depending on your configuration, you may choose a node to be a master for some data and slaves for others, or you may dedicate nodes for master or slave duties.

Using peer-to-peer replication and sharding is a common strategy for column-family databases. In a scenario like this you might have tens or hundreds of nodes in a cluster with data sharded over them. A good starting point for peer-to-peer replication is to have a replication factor of 3, so each shard is present on three nodes. Should a node fail, then the shards on that node will be built on the other nodes (see Figure 4.5).

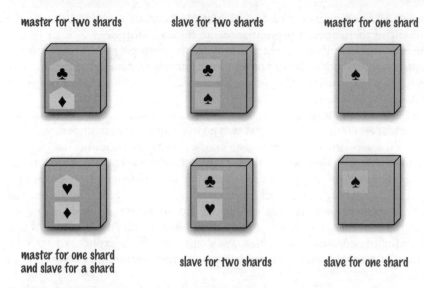

Figure 4.4   *Using master-slave replication together with sharding*

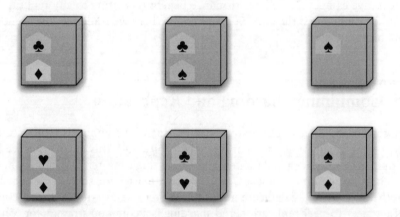

Figure 4.5   *Using peer-to-peer replication together with sharding*

4.6 Key Points

- There are two styles of distributing data:

  - Sharding distributes different data across multiple servers, so each server acts as the single source for a subset of data.

- Replication copies data across multiple servers, so each bit of data can be found in multiple places.

A system may use either or both techniques.

- Replication comes in two forms:

  - Master-slave replication makes one node the authoritative copy that handles writes while slaves synchronize with the master and may handle reads.

  - Peer-to-peer replication allows writes to any node; the nodes coordinate to synchronize their copies of the data.

Master-slave replication reduces the chance of update conflicts but peer-to-peer replication avoids loading all writes onto a single point of failure.

Chapter 5

Consistency

One of the biggest changes from a centralized relational database to a cluster-oriented NoSQL database is in how you think about consistency. Relational databases try to exhibit **strong consistency** by avoiding all the various inconsistencies that we'll shortly be discussing. Once you start looking at the NoSQL world, phrases such as "CAP theorem" and "eventual consistency" appear, and as soon as you start building something you have to think about what sort of consistency you need for your system.

Consistency comes in various forms, and that one word covers a myriad of ways errors can creep into your life. So we're going to begin by talking about the various shapes consistency can take. After that we'll discuss why you may want to relax consistency (and its big sister, durability).

5.1 Update Consistency

We'll begin by considering updating a telephone number. Coincidentally, Martin and Pramod are looking at the company website and notice that the phone number is out of date. Implausibly, they both have update access, so they both go in at the same time to update the number. To make the example interesting, we'll assume they update it slightly differently, because each uses a slightly different format. This issue is called a **write-write conflict**: two people updating the same data item at the same time.

When the writes reach the server, the server will **serialize** them—decide to apply one, then the other. Let's assume it uses alphabetical order and picks Martin's update first, then Pramod's. Without any concurrency control, Martin's update would be applied and immediately overwritten by Pramod's. In this case Martin's is a **lost update**. Here the lost update is not a big problem, but often it is. We see this as a failure of consistency because Pramod's update was based on the state before Martin's update, yet was applied after it.

Approaches for maintaining consistency in the face of concurrency are often described as pessimistic or optimistic. A **pessimistic** approach works by preventing conflicts from occurring; an **optimistic** approach lets conflicts occur, but detects them and takes action to sort them out. For update conflicts, the most common pessimistic approach is to have write locks, so that in order to change a value you need to acquire a lock, and the system ensures that only one client can get a lock at a time. So Martin and Pramod would both attempt to acquire the write lock, but only Martin (the first one) would succeed. Pramod would then see the result of Martin's write before deciding whether to make his own update.

A common optimistic approach is a **conditional update** where any client that does an update tests the value just before updating it to see if it's changed since his last read. In this case, Martin's update would succeed but Pramod's would fail. The error would let Pramod know that he should look at the value again and decide whether to attempt a further update.

Both the pessimistic and optimistic approaches that we've just described rely on a consistent serialization of the updates. With a single server, this is obvious—it has to choose one, then the other. But if there's more than one server, such as with peer-to-peer replication, then two nodes might apply the updates in a different order, resulting in a different value for the telephone number on each peer. Often, when people talk about concurrency in distributed systems, they talk about sequential consistency—ensuring that all nodes apply operations in the same order.

There is another optimistic way to handle a write-write conflict—save both updates and record that they are in conflict. This approach is familiar to many programmers from version control systems, particularly distributed version control systems that by their nature will often have conflicting commits. The next step again follows from version control: You have to merge the two updates somehow. Maybe you show both values to the user and ask them to sort it out—this is what happens if you update the same contact on your phone and your computer. Alternatively, the computer may be able to perform the merge itself; if it was a phone formatting issue, it may be able to realize that and apply the new number with the standard format. Any automated merge of write-write conflicts is highly domain-specific and needs to be programmed for each particular case.

Often, when people first encounter these issues, their reaction is to prefer pessimistic concurrency because they are determined to avoid conflicts. While in some cases this is the right answer, there is always a tradeoff. Concurrent programming involves a fundamental tradeoff between safety (avoiding errors such as update conflicts) and liveness (responding quickly to clients). Pessimistic approaches often severely degrade the responsiveness of a system to the degree that it becomes unfit for its purpose. This problem is made worse by the danger of errors—pessimistic concurrency often leads to deadlocks, which are hard to prevent and debug.

Replication makes it much more likely to run into write-write conflicts. If different nodes have different copies of some data which can be independently updated, then you'll get conflicts unless you take specific measures to avoid them. Using a single node as the target for all writes for some data makes it much easier to maintain update consistency. Of the distribution models we discussed earlier, all but peer-to-peer replication do this.

5.2 Read Consistency

Having a data store that maintains update consistency is one thing, but it doesn't guarantee that readers of that data store will always get consistent responses to their requests. Let's imagine we have an order with line items and a shipping charge. The shipping charge is calculated based on the line items in the order. If we add a line item, we thus also need to recalculate and update the shipping charge. In a relational database, the shipping charge and line items will be in separate tables. The danger of inconsistency is that Martin adds a line item to his order, Pramod then reads the line items and shipping charge, and then Martin updates the shipping charge. This is an **inconsistent read** or **read-write conflict**: In Figure 5.1 Pramod has done a read in the middle of Martin's write.

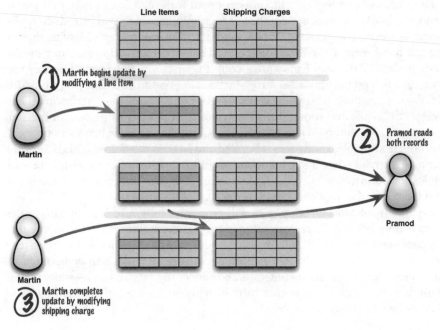

Figure 5.1   *A read-write conflict in logical consistency*

We refer to this type of consistency as **logical consistency**: ensuring that different data items make sense together. To avoid a logically inconsistent read-write conflict, relational databases support the notion of transactions. Providing Martin wraps his two writes in a transaction, the system guarantees that Pramod will either read both data items before the update or both after the update.

A common claim we hear is that NoSQL databases don't support transactions and thus can't be consistent. Such claim is mostly wrong because it glosses over lots of important details. Our first clarification is that any statement about lack of transactions usually only applies to some NoSQL databases, in particular the aggregate-oriented ones. In contrast, graph databases tend to support ACID transactions just the same as relational databases.

Secondly, aggregate-oriented databases do support atomic updates, but only within a single aggregate. This means that you will have logical consistency within an aggregate but not between aggregates. So in the example, you could avoid running into that inconsistency if the order, the delivery charge, and the line items are all part of a single order aggregate.

Of course not all data can be put in the same aggregate, so any update that affects multiple aggregates leaves open a time when clients could perform an inconsistent read. The length of time an inconsistency is present is called the **inconsistency window**. A NoSQL system may have a quite short inconsistency window: As one data point, Amazon's documentation says that the inconsistency window for its SimpleDB service is usually less than a second.

This example of a logically inconsistent read is the classic example that you'll see in any book that touches database programming. Once you introduce replication, however, you get a whole new kind of inconsistency. Let's imagine there's one last hotel room for a desirable event. The hotel reservation system runs on many nodes. Martin and Cindy are a couple considering this room, but they are discussing this on the phone because Martin is in London and Cindy is in Boston. Meanwhile Pramod, who is in Mumbai, goes and books that last room. That updates the replicated room availability, but the update gets to Boston quicker than it gets to London. When Martin and Cindy fire up their browsers to see if the room is available, Cindy sees it booked and Martin sees it free. This is another inconsistent read—but it's a breach of a different form of consistency we call **replication consistency**: ensuring that the same data item has the same value when read from different replicas (see Figure 5.2).

Eventually, of course, the updates will propagate fully, and Martin will see the room is fully booked. Therefore this situation is generally referred to as **eventually consistent**, meaning that at any time nodes may have replication inconsistencies but, if there are no further updates, eventually all nodes will be updated to the same value. Data that is out of date is generally referred to as **stale**, which reminds us that a cache is another form of replication—essentially following the master-slave distribution model.

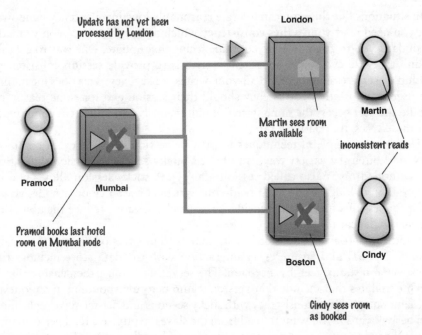

Figure 5.2 *An example of replication inconsistency*

Although replication consistency is independent from logical consistency, replication can exacerbate a logical inconsistency by lengthening its inconsistency window. Two different updates on the master may be performed in rapid succession, leaving an inconsistency window of milliseconds. But delays in networking could mean that the same inconsistency window lasts for much longer on a slave.

Consistency guarantees aren't something that's global to an application. You can usually specify the level of consistency you want with individual requests. This allows you to use weak consistency most of the time when it isn't an issue, but request strong consistency when it is.

The presence of an inconsistency window means that different people will see different things at the same time. If Martin and Cindy are looking at rooms while on a transatlantic call, it can cause confusion. It's more common for users to act independently, and then this is not a problem. But inconsistency windows can be particularly problematic when you get inconsistencies with yourself. Consider the example of posting comments on a blog entry. Few people are going to worry about inconsistency windows of even a few minutes while people are typing in their latest thoughts. Often, systems handle the load of such sites by running on a cluster and load-balancing incoming requests to different nodes. Therein lies a danger: You may post a message using one node, then refresh your browser, but the refresh goes to a different node which hasn't received your post yet—and it looks like your post was lost.

In situations like this, you can tolerate reasonably long inconsistency windows, but you need **read-your-writes consistency** which means that, once you've made an update, you're guaranteed to continue seeing that update. One way to get this in an otherwise eventually consistent system is to provide **session consistency**: Within a user's session there is read-your-writes consistency. This does mean that the user may lose that consistency should their session end for some reason or should the user access the same system simultaneously from different computers, but these cases are relatively rare.

There are a couple of techniques to provide session consistency. A common way, and often the easiest way, is to have a **sticky session**: a session that's tied to one node (this is also called **session affinity**). A sticky session allows you to ensure that as long as you keep read-your-writes consistency on a node, you'll get it for sessions too. The downside is that sticky sessions reduce the ability of the load balancer to do its job.

Another approach for session consistency is to use version stamps ("Version Stamps," p. 61) and ensure every interaction with the data store includes the latest version stamp seen by a session. The server node must then ensure that it has the updates that include that version stamp before responding to a request.

Maintaining session consistency with sticky sessions and master-slave replication can be awkward if you want to read from the slaves to improve read performance but still need to write to the master. One way of handling this is for writes to be sent to the slave, who then takes responsibility for forwarding them to the master while maintaining session consistency for its client. Another approach is to switch the session to the master temporarily when doing a write, just long enough that reads are done from the master until the slaves have caught up with the update.

We're talking about replication consistency in the context of a data store, but it's also an important factor in overall application design. Even a simple database system will have lots of occasions where data is presented to a user, the user cogitates, and then updates that data. It's usually a bad idea to keep a transaction open during user interaction because there's a real danger of conflicts when the user tries to make her update, which leads to such approaches as offline locks [Fowler PoEAA].

5.3 Relaxing Consistency

Consistency is a Good Thing—but, sadly, sometimes we have to sacrifice it. It is always possible to design a system to avoid inconsistencies, but often impossible to do so without making unbearable sacrifices in other characteristics of the system. As a result, we often have to tradeoff consistency for something else. While some architects see this as a disaster, we see it as part of the inevitable tradeoffs involved in system design. Furthermore, different domains have different tolerances for inconsistency, and we need to take this tolerance into account as we make our decisions.

Trading off consistency is a familiar concept even in single-server relational database systems. Here, our principal tool to enforce consistency is the transaction, and transactions can provide strong consistency guarantees. However, transaction systems usually come with the ability to relax isolation levels, allowing queries to read data that hasn't been committed yet, and in practice we see most applications relax consistency down from the highest isolation level (serialized) in order to get effective performance. We most commonly see people using the read-committed transaction level, which eliminates some read-write conflicts but allows others.

Many systems forgo transactions entirely because the performance impact of transactions is too high. We've seen this in a couple different ways. On a small scale, we saw the popularity of MySQL during the days when it didn't support transactions. Many websites liked the high speed of MySQL and were prepared to live without transactions. At the other end of the scale, some very large websites, such as eBay [Pritchett], have had to forgo transactions in order to perform acceptably—this is particularly true when you need to introduce sharding. Even without these constraints, many application builders need to interact with remote systems that can't be properly included within a transaction boundary, so updating outside of transactions is a quite common occurrence for enterprise applications.

5.3.1 The CAP Theorem

In the NoSQL world it's common to refer to the CAP theorem as the reason why you may need to relax consistency. It was originally proposed by Eric Brewer in 2000 [Brewer] and given a formal proof by Seth Gilbert and Nancy Lynch [Lynch and Gilbert] a couple of years later. (You may also hear this referred to as Brewer's Conjecture.)

The basic statement of the CAP theorem is that, given the three properties of Consistency, Availability, and Partition tolerance, you can only get two. Obviously this depends very much on how you define these three properties, and differing opinions have led to several debates on what the real consequences of the CAP theorem are.

Consistency is pretty much as we've defined it so far. **Availability** has a particular meaning in the context of CAP—it means that if you can talk to a node in the cluster, it can read and write data. That's subtly different from the usual meaning, which we'll explore later. **Partition tolerance** means that the cluster can survive communication breakages in the cluster that separate the cluster into multiple partitions unable to communicate with each other (situation known as a **split brain**, see Figure 5.3).

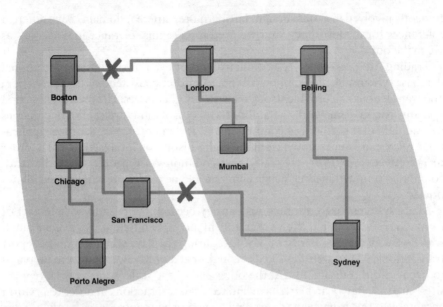

Figure 5.3 *With two breaks in the communication lines, the network partitions into two groups.*

A single-server system is the obvious example of a CA system—a system that has Consistency and Availability but not Partition tolerance. A single machine can't partition, so it does not have to worry about partition tolerance. There's only one node—so if it's up, it's available. Being up and keeping consistency is reasonable. This is the world that most relational database systems live in.

It is theoretically possible to have a CA cluster. However, this would mean that if a partition ever occurs in the cluster, all the nodes in the cluster would go down so that no client can talk to a node. By the usual definition of "available," this would mean a lack of availability, but this is where CAP's special usage of "availability" gets confusing. CAP defines "availability" to mean "every request received by a nonfailing node in the system must result in a response" [Lynch and Gilbert]. So a failed, unresponsive node doesn't infer a lack of CAP availability.

This does imply that you can build a CA cluster, but you have to ensure it will only partition rarely and completely. This can be done, at least within a data center, but it's usually prohibitively expensive. Remember that in order to bring down all the nodes in a cluster on a partition, you also have to detect the partition in a timely manner—which itself is no small feat.

So clusters have to be tolerant of network partitions. And here is the real point of the CAP theorem. Although the CAP theorem is often stated as "you can only get two out of three," in practice what it's saying is that in a system that may suffer partitions, as distributed system do, you have to trade off consistency versus availability. This isn't a binary decision; often, you can trade off a little consistency to get some availability. The resulting system would be neither perfectly consistent nor perfectly available—but would have a combination that is reasonable for your particular needs.

An example should help illustrate this. Martin and Pramod are both trying to book the last hotel room on a system that uses peer-to-peer distribution with two nodes (London for Martin and Mumbai for Pramod). If we want to ensure consistency, then when Martin tries to book his room on the London node, that node must communicate with the Mumbai node before confirming the booking. Essentially, both nodes must agree on the serialization of their requests. This gives us consistency—but should the network link break, then neither system can book any hotel room, sacrificing availability.

One way to improve availability is to designate one node as the master for a particular hotel and ensure all bookings are processed by that master. Should that master be Mumbai, then Mumbai can still process hotel bookings for that hotel and Pramod will get the last room. If we use master-slave replication, London users can see the inconsistent room information but cannot make a booking and thus cause an update inconsistency. However, users expect that it could happen in this situation—so, again, the compromise works for this particular use case.

This improves the situation, but we still can't book a room on the London node for the hotel whose master is in Mumbai if the connection goes down. In CAP terminology, this is a failure of availability in that Martin can talk to the London node but the London node cannot update the data. To gain more availability, we might allow both systems to keep accepting hotel reservations even if the network link breaks down. The danger here is that Martin and Pramod book the last hotel room. However, depending on how this hotel operates, that may be fine. Often, travel companies tolerate a certain amount of overbooking in order to cope with no-shows. Conversely, some hotels always keep a few rooms clear even when they are fully booked, in order to be able to swap a guest out of a room with problems or to accommodate a high-status late booking. Some might even cancel the booking with an apology once they detected the conflict—reasoning that the cost of that is less than the cost of losing bookings on network failures.

The classic example of allowing inconsistent writes is the shopping cart, as discussed in Dynamo [Amazon's Dynamo]. In this case you are always allowed to write to your shopping cart, even if network failures mean you end up with multiple shopping carts. The checkout process can merge the two shopping carts by putting the union of the items from the carts into a single cart and returning that. Almost always that's the correct answer—but if not, the user gets the opportunity to look at the cart before completing the order.

The lesson here is that although most software developers treat update consistency as The Way Things Must Be, there are cases where you can deal gracefully with inconsistent answers to requests. These situations are closely tied to the domain and require domain knowledge to know how to resolve. Thus you can't usually look to solve them purely within the development team—you have to talk to domain experts. If you can find a way to handle inconsistent updates, this gives you more options to increase availability and performance. For a shopping cart, it means that shoppers can always shop, and do so quickly. And as Patriotic Americans, we know how vital it is to support Our Retail Destiny.

A similar logic applies to read consistency. If you are trading financial instruments over a computerized exchange, you may not be able to tolerate any data that isn't right up to date. However, if you are posting a news item to a media website, you may be able to tolerate old pages for minutes.

In these cases you need to know how tolerant you are of stale reads, and how long the inconsistency window can be—often in terms of the average length, worst case, and some measure of the distribution for the lengths. Different data items may have different tolerances for staleness, and thus may need different settings in your replication configuration.

Advocates of NoSQL often say that instead of following the ACID properties of relational transactions, NoSQL systems follow the BASE properties (Basically Available, Soft state, Eventual consistency) [Brewer]. Although we feel we ought to mention the BASE acronym here, we don't think it's very useful. The acronym is even more contrived than ACID, and neither "basically available" nor "soft state" have been well defined. We should also stress that when Brewer introduced the notion of BASE, he saw the tradeoff between ACID and BASE as a spectrum, not a binary choice.

We've included this discussion of the CAP theorem because it's often used (and abused) when talking about the tradeoffs involving consistency in distributed databases. However, it's usually better to think not about the tradeoff between consistency and availability but rather between consistency and *latency*. We can summarize much of the discussion about consistency in distribution by saying that we can improve consistency by getting more nodes involved in the interaction, but each node we add increases the response time of that interaction. We can then think of availability as the limit of latency that we're prepared to tolerate; once latency gets too high, we give up and treat the data as unavailable—which neatly fits its definition in the context of CAP.

5.4 Relaxing Durability

So far we've talked about consistency, which is most of what people mean when they talk about the ACID properties of database transactions. The key to Consistency is serializing requests by forming Atomic, Isolated work units. But most people would scoff at relaxing durability—after all, what is the point of a data store if it can lose updates?

As it turns out, there are cases where you may want to trade off some durability for higher performance. If a database can run mostly in memory, apply updates to its in-memory representation, and periodically flush changes to disk, then it may be able to provide substantially higher responsiveness to requests. The cost is that, should the server crash, any updates since the last flush will be lost.

One example of where this tradeoff may be worthwhile is storing user-session state. A big website may have many users and keep temporary information about what each user is doing in some kind of session state. There's a lot of activity on this state, creating lots of demand, which affects the responsiveness of the website. The vital point is that losing the session data isn't too much of a tragedy—it will create some annoyance, but maybe less than a slower website would cause. This makes it a good candidate for nondurable writes. Often, you can specify the durability needs on a call-by-call basis, so that more important updates can force a flush to disk.

Another example of relaxing durability is capturing telemetric data from physical devices. It may be that you'd rather capture data at a faster rate, at the cost of missing the last updates should the server go down.

Another class of durability tradeoffs comes up with replicated data. A failure of **replication durability** occurs when a node processes an update but fails before that update is replicated to the other nodes. A simple case of this may happen if you have a master-slave distribution model where the slaves appoint a new master automatically should the existing master fail. If a master does fail, any writes not passed onto the replicas will effectively become lost. Should the master come back online, those updates will conflict with updates that have happened since. We think of this as a durability problem because you think your update has succeeded since the master acknowledged it, but a master node failure caused it to be lost.

If you're sufficiently confident in bringing the master back online rapidly, this is a reason not to auto-failover to a slave. Otherwise, you can improve replication durability by ensuring that the master waits for some replicas to acknowledge the update before the master acknowledges it to the client. Obviously, however, that will slow down updates and make the cluster unavailable if slaves fail—so, again, we have a tradeoff, depending upon how vital durability is. As with basic durability, it's useful for individual calls to indicate what level of durability they need.

5.5 Quorums

When you're trading off consistency or durability, it's not an all or nothing proposition. The more nodes you involve in a request, the higher is the chance of avoiding an inconsistency. This naturally leads to the question: How many nodes need to be involved to get strong consistency?

Imagine some data replicated over three nodes. You don't need all nodes to acknowledge a write to ensure strong consistency; all you need is two of them — a majority. If you have conflicting writes, only one can get a majority. This is referred to as a **write quorum** and expressed in a slightly pretentious inequality of $W > N/2$, meaning the number of nodes participating in the write (W) must be more than the half the number of nodes involved in replication (N). The number of replicas is often called the **replication factor**.

Similarly to the write quorum, there is the notion of read quorum: How many nodes you need to contact to be sure you have the most up-to-date change. The read quorum is a bit more complicated because it depends on how many nodes need to confirm a write.

Let's consider a replication factor of 3. If all writes need two nodes to confirm (W = 2) then we need to contact at least two nodes to be sure we'll get the latest data. If, however, writes are only confirmed by a single node (W = 1) we need to talk to all three nodes to be sure we have the latest updates. In this case, since we don't have a write quorum, we may have an update conflict, but by contacting enough readers we can be sure to detect it. Thus we can get strongly consistent reads even if we don't have strong consistency on our writes.

This relationship between the number of nodes you need to contact for a read (R), those confirming a write (W), and the replication factor (N) can be captured in an inequality: You can have a strongly consistent read if $R + W > N$.

These inequalities are written with a peer-to-peer distribution model in mind. If you have a master-slave distribution, you only have to write to the master to avoid write-write conflicts, and similarly only read from the master to avoid read-write conflicts. With this notation, it is common to confuse the number of nodes in the cluster with the replication factor, but these are often different. I may have 100 nodes in my cluster, but only have a replication factor of 3, with most of the distribution occurring due to sharding.

Indeed most authorities suggest that a replication factor of 3 is enough to have good resilience. This allows a single node to fail while still maintaining quora for reads and writes. If you have automatic rebalancing, it won't take too long for the cluster to create a third replica, so the chances of losing a second replica before a replacement comes up are slight.

The number of nodes participating in an operation can vary with the operation. When writing, we might require quorum for some types of updates but not others, depending on how much we value consistency and availability. Similarly, a read that needs speed but can tolerate staleness should contact less nodes.

Often you may need to take both into account. If you need fast, strongly consistent reads, you could require writes to be acknowledged by all the nodes, thus allowing reads to contact only one (N = 3, W = 3, R = 1). That would mean that your writes are slow, since they have to contact all three nodes, and you would not be able to tolerate losing a node. But in some circumstances that may be the tradeoff to make.

The point to all of this is that you have a range of options to work with and can choose which combination of problems and advantages to prefer. Some writers on NoSQL talk about a simple tradeoff between consistency and availability; we hope you now realize that it's more flexible—and more complicated—than that.

5.6 Further Reading

There are all sorts of interesting blog posts and papers on the Internet about consistency in distributed systems, but the most helpful source for us was [Tanenbaum and Van Steen]. It does an excellent job of organizing much of the fundamentals of distributed systems and is the best place to go if you'd like to delve deeper than we have in this chapter.

As we were finishing this book, *IEEE Computer* had a special issue [IEEE Computer Feb 2012] on the growing influence of the CAP theorem, which is a helpful source of further clarification for this topic.

5.7 Key Points

- Write-write conflicts occur when two clients try to write the same data at the same time. Read-write conflicts occur when one client reads inconsistent data in the middle of another client's write.

- Pessimistic approaches lock data records to prevent conflicts. Optimistic approaches detect conflicts and fix them.

- Distributed systems see read-write conflicts due to some nodes having received updates while other nodes have not. Eventual consistency means that at some point the system will become consistent once all the writes have propagated to all the nodes.

- Clients usually want read-your-writes consistency, which means a client can write and then immediately read the new value. This can be difficult if the read and the write happen on different nodes.

- To get good consistency, you need to involve many nodes in data operations, but this increases latency. So you often have to trade off consistency versus latency.

- The CAP theorem states that if you get a network partition, you have to trade off availability of data versus consistency.

- Durability can also be traded off against latency, particularly if you want to survive failures with replicated data.

- You do not need to contact all replicants to preserve strong consistency with replication; you just need a large enough quorum.

Chapter 6

Version Stamps

Many critics of NoSQL databases focus on the lack of support for transactions. Transactions are a useful tool that helps programmers support consistency. One reason why many NoSQL proponents worry less about a lack of transactions is that aggregate-oriented NoSQL databases do support atomic updates within an aggregate—and aggregates are designed so that their data forms a natural unit of update. That said, it's true that transactional needs are something to take into account when you decide what database to use.

As part of this, it's important to remember that transactions have limitations. Even within a transactional system we still have to deal with updates that require human intervention and usually cannot be run within transactions because they would involve holding a transaction open for too long. We can cope with these using **version stamps**—which turn out to be handy in other situations as well, particularly as we move away from the single-server distribution model.

6.1 Business and System Transactions

The need to support update consistency without transactions is actually a common feature of systems even when they are built on top of transactional databases. When users think about transactions, they usually mean **business transactions**. A business transaction may be something like browsing a product catalog, choosing a bottle of Talisker at a good price, filling in credit card information, and confirming the order. Yet all of this usually won't occur within the **system transaction** provided by the database because this would mean locking the database elements while the user is trying to find their credit card and gets called off to lunch by their colleagues.

Usually applications only begin a system transaction at the end of the interaction with the user, so that the locks are only held for a short period of time. The problem, however, is that calculations and decisions may have been made based on data that's changed. The price list may have updated the price of the Talisker, or someone may have updated the customer's address, changing the shipping charges.

The broad techniques for handling this are offline concurrency [Fowler PoEAA], useful in NoSQL situations too. A particularly useful approach is the Optimistic Offline Lock [Fowler PoEAA], a form of conditional update where a client operation rereads any information that the business transaction relies on and checks that it hasn't changed since it was originally read and displayed to the user. A good way of doing this is to ensure that records in the database contain some form of **version stamp**: a field that changes every time the underlying data in the record changes. When you read the data you keep a note of the version stamp, so that when you write data you can check to see if the version has changed.

You may have come across this technique with updating resources with HTTP [HTTP]. One way of doing this is to use etags. Whenever you get a resource, the server responds with an etag in the header. This etag is an opaque string that indicates the version of the resource. If you then update that resource, you can use a conditional update by supplying the etag that you got from your last GET. If the resource has changed on the server, the etags won't match and the server will refuse the update, returning a 412 (Precondition Failed) response.

Some databases provide a similar mechanism of conditional update that allows you to ensure updates won't be based on stale data. You can do this check yourself, although you then have to ensure no other thread can run against the resource between your read and your update. (Sometimes this is called a compare-and-set (CAS) operation, whose name comes from the CAS operations done in processors. The difference is that a processor CAS compares a value before setting it, while a database conditional update compares a version stamp of the value.)

There are various ways you can construct your version stamps. You can use a counter, always incrementing it when you update the resource. Counters are useful since they make it easy to tell if one version is more recent than another. On the other hand, they require the server to generate the counter value, and also need a single master to ensure the counters aren't duplicated.

Another approach is to create a GUID, a large random number that's guaranteed to be unique. These use some combination of dates, hardware information, and whatever other sources of randomness they can pick up. The nice thing about GUIDs is that they can be generated by anyone and you'll never get a duplicate; a disadvantage is that they are large and can't be compared directly for recentness.

A third approach is to make a hash of the contents of the resource. With a big enough hash key size, a content hash can be globally unique like a GUID and can also be generated by anyone; the advantage is that they are deterministic—any node will generate the same content hash for same resource data. However, like GUIDs they can't be directly compared for recentness, and they can be lengthy.

A fourth approach is to use the timestamp of the last update. Like counters, they are reasonably short and can be directly compared for recentness, yet have the advantage of not needing a single master. Multiple machines can generate timestamps—but to work properly, their clocks have to be kept in sync. One node with a bad clock can cause all sorts of data corruptions. There's also a danger that if the timestamp is too granular you can get duplicates—it's no good using timestamps of a millisecond precision if you get many updates per millisecond.

You can blend the advantages of these different version stamp schemes by using more than one of them to create a composite stamp. For example, CouchDB uses a combination of counter and content hash. Most of the time this allows version stamps to be compared for recentness, even when you use peer-to-peer replication. Should two peers update at the same time, the combination of the same count and different content hashes makes it easy to spot the conflict.

As well as helping to avoid update conflicts, version stamps are also useful for providing session consistency (p. 52).

6.2 Version Stamps on Multiple Nodes

The basic version stamp works well when you have a single authoritative source for data, such as a single server or master-slave replication. In that case the version stamp is controlled by the master. Any slaves follow the master's stamps. But this system has to be enhanced in a peer-to-peer distribution model because there's no longer a single place to set the version stamps.

If you're asking two nodes for some data, you run into the chance that they may give you different answers. If this happens, your reaction may vary depending on the cause of that difference. It may be that an update has only reached one node but not the other, in which case you can accept the latest (assuming you can tell which one that is). Alternatively, you may have run into an inconsistent update, in which case you need to decide how to deal with that. In this situation, a simple GUID or etag won't suffice, since these don't tell you enough about the relationships.

The simplest form of version stamp is a counter. Each time a node updates the data, it increments the counter and puts the value of the counter into the version stamp. If you have blue and green slave replicas of a single master, and the blue node answers with a version stamp of 4 and the green node with 6, you know that the green's answer is more recent.

In multiple-master cases, we need something fancier. One approach, used by distributed version control systems, is to ensure that all nodes contain a history of version stamps. That way you can see if the blue node's answer is an ancestor of the green's answer. This would either require the clients to hold onto version stamp histories, or the server nodes to keep version stamp histories and include them when asked for data. This also detects an inconsistency, which we would see if we get two version stamps and neither of them has the other in their histories. Although version control systems keep these kinds of histories, they aren't found in NoSQL databases.

A simple but problematic approach is to use timestamps. The main problem here is that it's usually difficult to ensure that all the nodes have a consistent notion of time, particularly if updates can happen rapidly. Should a node's clock get out of sync, it can cause all sorts of trouble. In addition, you can't detect write-write conflicts with timestamps, so it would only work well for the single-master case—and then a counter is usually better.

The most common approach used by peer-to-peer NoSQL systems is a special form of version stamp which we call a vector stamp. In essence, a **vector stamp** is a set of counters, one for each node. A vector stamp for three nodes (blue, green, black) would look something like [blue: 43, green: 54, black: 12]. Each time a node has an internal update, it updates its own counter, so an update in the green node would change the vector to [blue: 43, green: 55, black: 12]. Whenever two nodes communicate, they synchronize their vector stamps. There are several variations of exactly how this synchronization is done. We're coining the term "vector stamp" as a general term in this book; you'll also come across **vector clocks** and **version vectors**—these are specific forms of vector stamps that differ in how they synchronize.

By using this scheme you can tell if one version stamp is newer than another because the newer stamp will have all its counters greater than or equal to those in the older stamp. So [blue: 1, green: 2, black: 5] is newer than [blue:1, green: 1, black 5] since one of its counters is greater. If both stamps have a counter greater than the other, e.g. [blue: 1, green: 2, black: 5] and [blue: 2, green: 1, black: 5], then you have a write-write conflict.

There may be missing values in the vector, in which case we treat the missing value as 0. So [blue: 6, black: 2] would be treated as [blue: 6, green: 0, black: 2]. This allows you to easily add new nodes without invalidating the existing vector stamps.

Vector stamps are a valuable tool that spots inconsistencies, but doesn't resolve them. Any conflict resolution will depend on the domain you are working in. This is part of the consistency/latency tradeoff. You either have to live with the fact that network partitions may make your system unavailable, or you have to detect and deal with inconsistencies.

6.3 Key Points

- Version stamps help you detect concurrency conflicts. When you read data, then update it, you can check the version stamp to ensure nobody updated the data between your read and write.

- Version stamps can be implemented using counters, GUIDs, content hashes, timestamps, or a combination of these.

- With distributed systems, a vector of version stamps allows you to detect when different nodes have conflicting updates.

Chapter 7

Map-Reduce

The rise of aggregate-oriented databases is in large part due to the growth of clusters. Running on a cluster means you have to make your tradeoffs in data storage differently than when running on a single machine. Clusters don't just change the rules for data storage—they also change the rules for computation. If you store lots of data on a cluster, processing that data efficiently means you have to think differently about how you organize your processing.

With a centralized database, there are generally two ways you can run the processing logic against it: either on the database server itself or on a client machine. Running it on a client machine gives you more flexibility in choosing a programming environment, which usually makes for programs that are easier to create or extend. This comes at the cost of having to shlep lots of data from the database server. If you need to hit a lot of data, then it makes sense to do the processing on the server, paying the price in programming convenience and increasing the load on the database server.

When you have a cluster, there is good news immediately—you have lots of machines to spread the computation over. However, you also still need to try to reduce the amount of data that needs to be transferred across the network by doing as much processing as you can on the same node as the data it needs.

The map-reduce pattern (a form of *Scatter-Gather* [Hohpe and Woolf]) is a way to organize processing in such a way as to take advantage of multiple machines on a cluster while keeping as much processing and the data it needs together on the same machine. It first gained prominence with Google's MapReduce framework [Dean and Ghemawat]. A widely used open-source implementation is part of the Hadoop project, although several databases include their own implementations. As with most patterns, there are differences in detail between these implementations, so we'll concentrate on the general concept. The name "map-reduce" reveals its inspiration from the map and reduce operations on collections in functional programming languages.

7.1 Basic Map-Reduce

To explain the basic idea, we'll start from an example we've already flogged to death—that of customers and orders. Let's assume we have chosen orders as our aggregate, with each order having line items. Each line item has a product ID, quantity, and the price charged. This aggregate makes a lot of sense as usually people want to see the whole order in one access. We have lots of orders, so we've sharded the dataset over many machines.

However, sales analysis people want to see a product and its total revenue for the last seven days. This report doesn't fit the aggregate structure that we have—which is the downside of using aggregates. In order to get the product revenue report, you'll have to visit every machine in the cluster and examine many records on each machine.

This is exactly the kind of situation that calls for map-reduce. The first stage in a map-reduce job is the map. A map is a function whose input is a single aggregate and whose output is a bunch of key-value pairs. In this case, the input would be an order. The output would be key-value pairs corresponding to the line items. Each one would have the product ID as the key and an embedded map with the quantity and price as the values (see Figure 7.1).

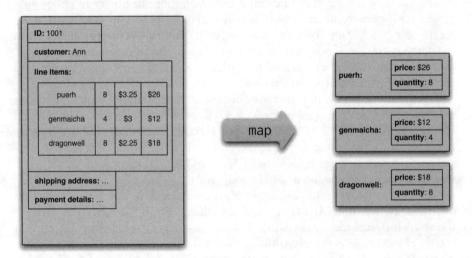

Figure 7.1   *A map function reads records from the database and emits key-value pairs.*

Each application of the map function is independent of all the others. This allows them to be safely parallelizable, so that a map-reduce framework can create efficient map tasks on each node and freely allocate each order to a map task. This yields a great deal of parallelism and locality of data access. For this example, we are just selecting a value out of the record, but there's no reason why we can't carry out some arbitrarily complex function as part of the map—providing it only depends on one aggregate's worth of data.

A map operation only operates on a single record; the reduce function takes multiple map outputs with the same key and combines their values. So, a map function might yield 1000 line items from orders for "Database Refactoring"; the reduce function would reduce down to one, with the totals for the quantity and revenue. While the map function is limited to working only on data from a single aggregate, the reduce function can use all values emitted for a single key (see Figure 7.2).

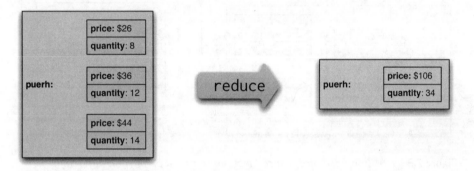

Figure 7.2 *A reduce function takes several key-value pairs with the same key and aggregates them into one.*

The map-reduce framework arranges for map tasks to be run on the correct nodes to process all the documents and for data to be moved to the reduce function. To make it easier to write the reduce function, the framework collects all the values for a single pair and calls the reduce function once with the key and the collection of all the values for that key. So to run a map-reduce job, you just need to write these two functions.

7.2 Partitioning and Combining

In the simplest form, we think of a map-reduce job as having a single reduce function. The outputs from all the map tasks running on the various nodes are concatenated together and sent into the reduce. While this will work, there are things we can do to increase the parallelism and to reduce the data transfer (see Figure 7.3).

The first thing we can do is increase parallelism by partitioning the output of the mappers. Each reduce function operates on the results of a single key. This

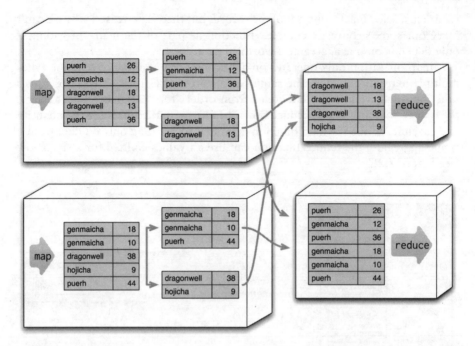

Figure 7.3 *Partitioning allows reduce functions to run in parallel on different keys.*

is a limitation—it means you can't do anything in the reduce that operates across keys—but it's also a benefit in that it allows you to run multiple reducers in parallel. To take advantage of this, the results of the mapper are divided up based on the key of each processing node. Typically, multiple keys are grouped together into partitions. The framework then takes the data from all the nodes for one partition, combines it into a single group for that partition, and sends it off to a reducer. Multiple reducers can then operate on the partitions in parallel, with the final results merged together. (This step is also called "shuffling," and the partitions are sometimes referred to as "buckets" or "regions.")

The next problem we can deal with is the amount of data being moved from node to node between the map and reduce stages. Much of this data is repetitive, consisting of multiple key-value pairs for the same key. A combiner function cuts this data down by combining all the data for the same key into a single value (see Figure 7.4). A combiner function is, in essence, a reducer function—indeed, in many cases the same function can be used for combining as the final reduction. The reduce function needs a special shape for this to work: Its output must match its input. We call such a function a **combinable reducer**.

Not all reduce functions are combinable. Consider a function that counts the number of unique customers for a particular product. The map function for such an operation would need to emit the product and the customer. The reducer can then combine them and count how many times each customer appears for a

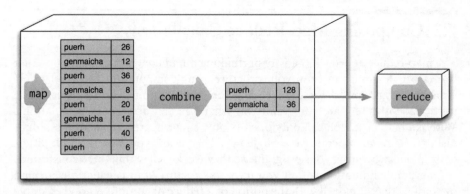

Figure 7.4 *Combining reduces data before sending it across the network.*

particular product, emitting the product and the count (see Figure 7.5). But this reducer's output is different from its input, so it can't be used as a combiner. You can still run a combining function here: one that just eliminates duplicate product-customer pairs, but it will be different from the final reducer.

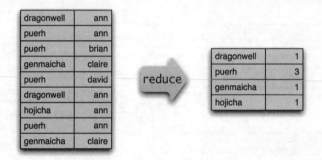

Figure 7.5 *This reduce function, which counts how many unique customers order a particular tea, is not combinable.*

When you have combining reducers, the map-reduce framework can safely run not only in parallel (to reduce different partitions), but also in series to reduce the same partition at different times and places. In addition to allowing combining to occur on a node before data transmission, you can also start combining before mappers have finished. This provides a good bit of extra flexibility to the map-reduce processing. Some map-reduce frameworks require all reducers to be combining reducers, which maximizes this flexibility. If you need to do a noncombining reducer with one of these frameworks, you'll need to separate the processing into pipelined map-reduce steps.

7.3 Composing Map-Reduce Calculations

The map-reduce approach is a way of thinking about concurrent processing that trades off flexibility in how you structure your computation for a relatively straightforward model for parallelizing the computation over a cluster. Since it's a tradeoff, there are constraints on what you can do in your calculations. Within a map task, you can only operate on a single aggregate. Within a reduce task, you can only operate on a single key. This means you have to think differently about structuring your programs so they work well within these constraints.

One simple limitation is that you have to structure your calculations around operations that fit in well with the notion of a reduce operation. A good example of this is calculating averages. Let's consider the kind of orders we've been looking at so far; suppose we want to know the average ordered quantity of each product. An important property of averages is that they are not composable—that is, if I take two groups of orders, I can't combine their averages alone. Instead, I need to take total amount and the count of orders from each group, combine those, and then calculate the average from the combined sum and count (see Figure 7.6).

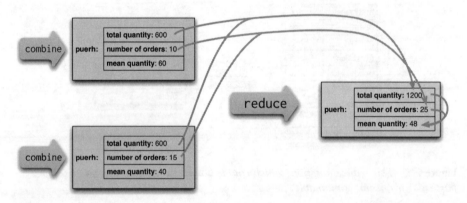

Figure 7.6 *When calculating averages, the sum and count can be combined in the reduce calculation, but the average must be calculated from the combined sum and count.*

This notion of looking for calculations that reduce neatly also affects how we do counts. To make a count, the mapping function will emit count fields with a value of 1, which can be summed to get a total count (see Figure 7.7).

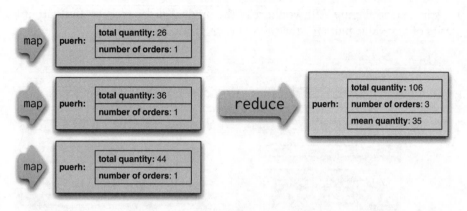

Figure 7.7   *When making a count, each map emits 1, which can be summed to get a total.*

7.3.1 A Two Stage Map-Reduce Example

As map-reduce calculations get more complex, it's useful to break them down into stages using a pipes-and-filters approach, with the output of one stage serving as input to the next, rather like the pipelines in UNIX.

Consider an example where we want to compare the sales of products for each month in 2011 to the prior year. To do this, we'll break the calculations down into two stages. The first stage will produce records showing the aggregate figures for a single product in a single month of the year. The second stage then uses these as inputs and produces the result for a single product by comparing one month's results with the same month in the prior year (see Figure 7.8).

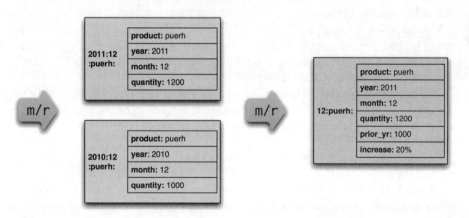

Figure 7.8   *A calculation broken down into two map-reduce steps, which will be expanded in the next three figures*

A first stage (Figure 7.9) would read the original order records and output a series of key-value pairs for the sales of each product per month.

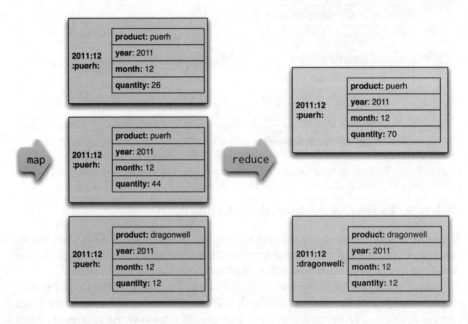

Figure 7.9   *Creating records for monthly sales of a product*

This stage is similar to the map-reduce examples we've seen so far. The only new feature is using a composite key so that we can reduce records based on the values of multiple fields.

The second-stage mappers (Figure 7.10) process this output depending on the year. A 2011 record populates the current year quantity while a 2010 record populates a prior year quantity. Records for earlier years (such as 2009) don't result in any mapping output being emitted.

The reduce in this case (Figure 7.11) is a merge of records, where combining the values by summing allows two different year outputs to be reduced to a single value (with a calculation based on the reduced values thrown in for good measure).

Decomposing this report into multiple map-reduce steps makes it easier to write. Like many transformation examples, once you've found a transformation framework that makes it easy to compose steps, it's usually easier to compose many small steps together than try to cram heaps of logic into a single step.

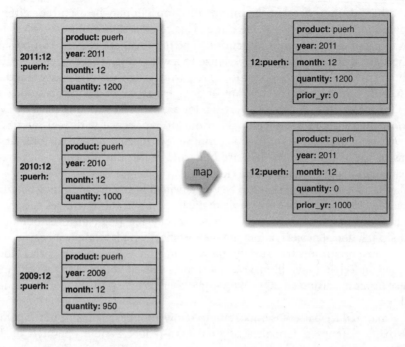

Figure 7.10 *The second stage mapper creates base records for year-on-year comparisons.*

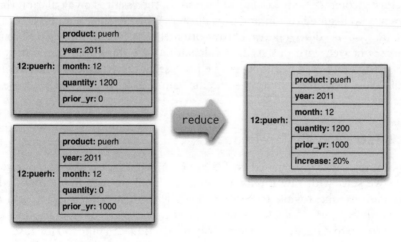

Figure 7.11 *The reduction step is a merge of incomplete records.*

Another advantage is that the intermediate output may be useful for different outputs too, so you can get some reuse. This reuse is important as it saves time both in programming and in execution. The intermediate records can be saved in the data store, forming a materialized view ("Materialized Views," p. 30). Early stages of map-reduce operations are particularly valuable to save since they often represent the heaviest amount of data access, so building them once as a basis for many downstream uses saves a lot of work. As with any reuse activity, however, it's important to build them out of experience with real queries, as speculative reuse rarely fulfills its promise. So it's important to look at the forms of various queries as they are built and factor out the common parts of the calculations into materialized views.

Map-reduce is a pattern that can be implemented in any programming language. However, the constraints of the style make it a good fit for languages specifically designed for map-reduce computations. Apache Pig [Pig], an offshoot of the Hadoop [Hadoop] project, is a language specifically built to make it easy to write map-reduce programs. It certainly makes it much easier to work with Hadoop than the underlying Java libraries. In a similar vein, if you want to specify map-reduce programs using an SQL-like syntax, there is hive [Hive], another Hadoop offshoot.

The map-reduce pattern is important to know about even outside of the context of NoSQL databases. Google's original map-reduce system operated on files stored on a distributed file system—an approach that's used by the open-source Hadoop project. While it takes some thought to get used to the constraints of structuring computations in map-reduce steps, the result is a calculation that is inherently well-suited to running on a cluster. When dealing with high volumes of data, you need to take a cluster-oriented approach. Aggregate-oriented databases fit well with this style of calculation. We think that in the next few years many more organizations will be processing the volumes of data that demand a cluster-oriented solution—and the map-reduce pattern will see more and more use.

7.3.2 Incremental Map-Reduce

The examples we've discussed so far are complete map-reduce computations, where we start with raw inputs and create a final output. Many map-reduce computations take a while to perform, even with clustered hardware, and new data keeps coming in which means we need to rerun the computation to keep the output up to date. Starting from scratch each time can take too long, so often it's useful to structure a map-reduce computation to allow incremental updates, so that only the minimum computation needs to be done.

The map stages of a map-reduce are easy to handle incrementally—only if the input data changes does the mapper need to be rerun. Since maps are isolated from each other, incremental updates are straightforward.

The more complex case is the reduce step, since it pulls together the outputs from many maps and any change in the map outputs could trigger a new reduction. This recomputation can be lessened depending on how parallel the reduce step is. If we are partitioning the data for reduction, then any partition that's unchanged does not need to be re-reduced. Similarly, if there's a combiner step, it doesn't need to be rerun if its source data hasn't changed.

If our reducer is combinable, there's some more opportunities for computation avoidance. If the changes are additive—that is, if we are only adding new records but are not changing or deleting any old records—then we can just run the reduce with the existing result and the new additions. If there are destructive changes, that is updates and deletes, then we can avoid some recomputation by breaking up the reduce operation into steps and only recalculating those steps whose inputs have changed—essentially, using a *Dependency Network* [Fowler DSL] to organize the computation.

The map-reduce framework controls much of this, so you have to understand how a specific framework supports incremental operation.

7.4 Further Reading

If you're going to use map-reduce calculations, your first port of call will be the documentation for the particular database you are using. Each database has its own approach, vocabulary, and quirks, and that's what you'll need to be familiar with. Beyond that, there is a need to capture more general information on how to structure map-reduce jobs to maximize maintainability and performance. We don't have any specific books to point to yet, but we suspect that a good though easily overlooked source are books on Hadoop. Although Hadoop is not a database, it's a tool that uses map-reduce heavily, so writing an effective map-reduce task with Hadoop is likely to be useful in other contexts (subject to the changes in detail between Hadoop and whatever systems you're using).

7.5 Key Points

- Map-reduce is a pattern to allow computations to be parallelized over a cluster.

- The map task reads data from an aggregate and boils it down to relevant key-value pairs. Maps only read a single record at a time and can thus be parallelized and run on the node that stores the record.

- Reduce tasks take many values for a single key output from map tasks and summarize them into a single output. Each reducer operates on the result of a single key, so it can be parallelized by key.

- Reducers that have the same form for input and output can be combined into pipelines. This improves parallelism and reduces the amount of data to be transferred.

- Map-reduce operations can be composed into pipelines where the output of one reduce is the input to another operation's map.

- If the result of a map-reduce computation is widely used, it can be stored as a materialized view.

- Materialized views can be updated through incremental map-reduce operations that only compute changes to the view instead of recomputing everything from scratch.

Part II

Implement

Chapter 8

Key-Value Databases

A key-value store is a simple hash table, primarily used when all access to the database is via primary key. Think of a table in a traditional RDBMS with two columns, such as ID and NAME, the ID column being the key and NAME column storing the value. In an RDBMS, the NAME column is restricted to storing data of type String. The application can provide an ID and VALUE and persist the pair; if the ID already exists the current value is overwritten, otherwise a new entry is created. Let's look at how terminology compares in Oracle and Riak.

Oracle	Riak
database instance	Riak cluster
table	bucket
row	key-value
rowid	key

8.1 What Is a Key-Value Store

Key-value stores are the simplest NoSQL data stores to use from an API perspective. The client can either get the value for the key, put a value for a key, or delete a key from the data store. The value is a blob that the data store just stores, without caring or knowing what's inside; it's the responsibility of the application to understand what was stored. Since key-value stores always use primary-key access, they generally have great performance and can be easily scaled.

Some of the popular key-value databases are Riak [Riak], Redis (often referred to as Data Structure server) [Redis], Memcached DB and its flavors [Memcached], Berkeley DB [Berkeley DB], HamsterDB (especially suited for embedded use)

[HamsterDB], Amazon DynamoDB [Amazon's Dynamo] (not open-source), and Project Voldemort [Project Voldemort] (an open-source implementation of Amazon DynamoDB).

In some key-value stores, such as Redis, the aggregate being stored does not have to be a domain object—it could be any data structure. Redis supports storing `lists`, `sets`, `hashes` and can do range, diff, union, and intersection operations. These features allow Redis to be used in more different ways than a standard key-value store.

There are many more key-value databases and many new ones are being worked on at this time. For the sake of keeping discussions in this book easier we will focus mostly on Riak. Riak lets us store keys into buckets, which are just a way to segment the keys—think of buckets as flat namespaces for the keys.

If we wanted to store user session data, shopping cart information, and user preferences in Riak, we could just store all of them in the same bucket with a single key and single value for all of these objects. In this scenario, we would have a single object that stores all the data and is put into a single bucket (Figure 8.1).

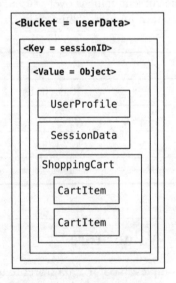

Figure 8.1 *Storing all the data in a single bucket*

The downside of storing all the different objects (aggregates) in the single bucket would be that one bucket would store different types of aggregates, increasing the chance of key conflicts. An alternate approach would be to append the name of the object to the key, such as `288790b8a421_userProfile`, so that we can get to individual objects as they are needed (Figure 8.2).

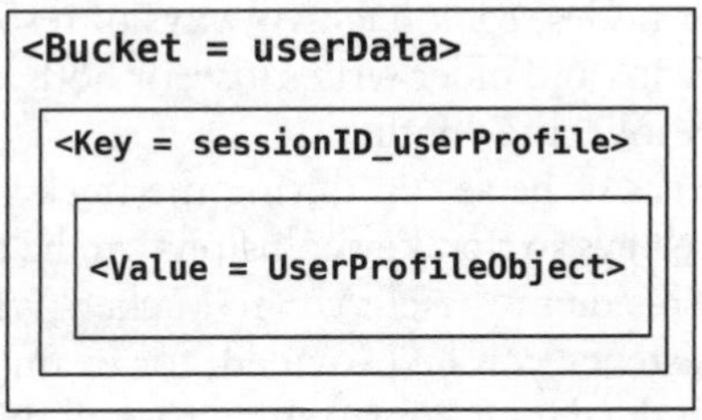

```
<Bucket = userData>

  <Key = sessionID_userProfile>

    <Value = UserProfileObject>
```

Figure 8.2 *Change the key design to segment the data in a single bucket.*

We could also create buckets which store specific data. In Riak, they are known as **domain buckets** allowing the serialization and deserialization to be handled by the client driver.

```
Bucket bucket = client.fetchBucket(bucketName).execute();
DomainBucket<UserProfile> profileBucket =
DomainBucket.builder(bucket, UserProfile.class).build();
```

Using domain buckets or different buckets for different objects (such as `UserProfile` and `ShoppingCart`) segments the data across different buckets allowing you to read only the object you need without having to change key design.

Key-value stores such as Redis also support storing random data structures, which can be sets, hashes, strings, and so on. This feature can be used to store lists of things, like `states` or `addressTypes`, or an array of user's visits.

8.2 Key-Value Store Features

While using any NoSQL data stores, there is an inevitable need to understand how the features compare to the standard RDBMS data stores that we are so used to. The primary reason is to understand what features are missing and how does the application architecture need to change to better use the features of a key-value data store. Some of the features we will discuss for all the NoSQL data stores are consistency, transactions, query features, structure of the data, and scaling.

8.2.1 Consistency

Consistency is applicable only for operations on a single key, since these operations are either a get, put, or delete on a single key. Optimistic writes can be performed, but are very expensive to implement, because a change in value cannot be determined by the data store.

In distributed key-value store implementations like Riak, the *eventually consistent* (p. 50) model of consistency is implemented. Since the value may have already been replicated to other nodes, Riak has two ways of resolving update conflicts: either the newest write wins and older writes lose, or both (all) values are returned allowing the client to resolve the conflict.

In Riak, these options can be set up during the bucket creation. Buckets are just a way to namespace keys so that key collisions can be reduced—for example, all customer keys may reside in the `customer` bucket. When creating a bucket, default values for consistency can be provided, for example that a write is considered good only when the data is consistent across all the nodes where the data is stored.

```
Bucket bucket = connection
    .createBucket(bucketName)
    .withRetrier(attempts(3))
    .allowSiblings(siblingsAllowed)
    .nVal(numberOfReplicasOfTheData)
    .w(numberOfNodesToRespondToWrite)
    .r(numberOfNodesToRespondToRead)
    .execute();
```

If we need data in every node to be consistent, we can increase the `numberOfNodesToRespondToWrite` set by `w` to be the same as `nVal`. Of course doing that will decrease the write performance of the cluster. To improve on write or read conflicts, we can change the `allowSiblings` flag during bucket creation: If it is set to false, we let the last write to win and not create siblings.

8.2.2 Transactions

Different products of the key-value store kind have different specifications of transactions. Generally speaking, there are no guarantees on the writes. Many data stores do implement transactions in different ways. Riak uses the concept of quorum ("Quorums," p. 57) implemented by using the W value—write quorum—during the write API call.

Assume we have a Riak cluster with a replication factor of 5 and we supply the W value of 3. When writing, the write is reported as successful only when it is written and reported as a success on at least three of the nodes. This allows Riak to have write tolerance; in our example, with N equal to 5 and with a W value of 3, the cluster can tolerate N - W = 2 nodes being down for write operations, though we would still have lost some data on those nodes for read.

8.2.3 Query Features

All key-value stores can query by the key—and that's about it. If you have requirements to query by using some attribute of the value column, it's not possible to use the database: Your application needs to read the value to figure out if the attribute meets the conditions.

Query by key also has an interesting side effect. What if we don't know the key, especially during ad-hoc querying during debugging? Most of the data stores will not give you a list of all the primary keys; even if they did, retrieving lists of keys and then querying for the value would be very cumbersome. Some key-value databases get around this by providing the ability to search inside the value, such as **Riak Search** that allows you to query the data just like you would query it using Lucene indexes.

While using key-value stores, lots of thought has to be given to the design of the key. Can the key be generated using some algorithm? Can the key be provided by the user (user ID, email, etc.)? Or derived from timestamps or other data that can be derived outside of the database?

These query characteristics make key-value stores likely candidates for storing session data (with the session ID as the key), shopping cart data, user profiles, and so on. The `expiry_secs` property can be used to expire keys after a certain time interval, especially for session/shopping cart objects.

```
Bucket bucket = getBucket(bucketName);
IRiakObject riakObject = bucket.store(key, value).execute();
```

When writing to the Riak bucket using the `store` API, the object is stored for the key provided. Similarly, we can get the value stored for the key using the `fetch` API.

```
Bucket bucket = getBucket(bucketName);
IRiakObject riakObject = bucket.fetch(key).execute();
byte[] bytes = riakObject.getValue();
String value = new String(bytes);
```

Riak provides an HTTP-based interface, so that all operations can be performed from the web browser or on the command line using `curl`. Let's save this data to Riak:

```
{
"lastVisit":1324669989288,
"user":{
  "customerId":"91cfdf5bcb7c",
  "name":"buyer",
  "countryCode":"US",
  "tzOffset":0
  }
}
```

Use the `curl` command to `POST` the data, storing the data in the `session` bucket with the key of `a7e618d9db25` (we have to provide this key):

```
curl -v -X POST -d '
{ "lastVisit":1324669989288,
  "user":{"customerId":"91cfdf5bcb7c",
  "name":"buyer",
  "countryCode":"US",
  "tzOffset":0}
}'
-H "Content-Type: application/json"
http://localhost:8098/buckets/session/keys/a7e618d9db25
```

The data for the key a7e618d9db25 can be fetched by using the curl command:

```
curl -i http://localhost:8098/buckets/session/keys/a7e618d9db25
```

8.2.4 Structure of Data

Key-value databases don't care what is stored in the value part of the key-value pair. The value can be a blob, text, JSON, XML, and so on. In Riak, we can use the Content-Type in the POST request to specify the data type.

8.2.5 Scaling

Many key-value stores scale by using sharding ("Sharding," p. 38). With sharding, the value of the key determines on which node the key is stored. Let's assume we are sharding by the first character of the key; if the key is f4b19d79587d, which starts with an f, it will be sent to different node than the key ad9c7a396542. This kind of sharding setup can increase performance as more nodes are added to the cluster.

Sharding also introduces some problems. If the node used to store f goes down, the data stored on that node becomes unavailable, nor can new data be written with keys that start with f.

Data stores such as Riak allow you to control the aspects of the CAP Theorem ("The CAP Theorem," p. 53): N (number of nodes to store the key-value replicas), R (number of nodes that have to have the data being fetched before the read is considered successful), and W (the number of nodes the write has to be written to before it is considered successful).

Let's assume we have a 5-node Riak cluster. Setting N to 3 means that all data is replicated to at least three nodes, setting R to 2 means any two nodes must reply to a GET request for it to be considered successful, and setting W to 2 ensures that the PUT request is written to two nodes before the write is considered successful.

These settings allow us to fine-tune node failures for read or write operations. Based on our need, we can change these values for better read availability or write availability. Generally speaking choose a W value to match your consistency needs; these values can be set as defaults during bucket creation.

8.3 Suitable Use Cases

Let's discuss some of the problems where key-value stores are a good fit.

8.3.1 Storing Session Information

Generally, every web session is unique and is assigned a unique `sessionid` value. Applications that store the `sessionid` on disk or in an RDBMS will greatly benefit from moving to a key-value store, since everything about the session can be stored by a single `PUT` request or retrieved using `GET`. This single-request operation makes it very fast, as everything about the session is stored in a single object. Solutions such as Memcached are used by many web applications, and Riak can be used when availability is important.

8.3.2 User Profiles, Preferences

Almost every user has a unique `userId`, `username`, or some other attribute, as well as preferences such as language, color, timezone, which products the user has access to, and so on. This can all be put into an object, so getting preferences of a user takes a single `GET` operation. Similarly, product profiles can be stored.

8.3.3 Shopping Cart Data

E-commerce websites have shopping carts tied to the user. As we want the shopping carts to be available all the time, across browsers, machines, and sessions, all the shopping information can be put into the `value` where the key is the `userid`. A Riak cluster would be best suited for these kinds of applications.

8.4 When Not to Use

There are problem spaces where key-value stores are not the best solution.

8.4.1 Relationships among Data

If you need to have relationships between different sets of data, or correlate the data between different sets of keys, key-value stores are not the best solution to use, even though some key-value stores provide link-walking features.

8.4.2 Multioperation Transactions

If you're saving multiple keys and there is a failure to save any one of them, and you want to revert or roll back the rest of the operations, key-value stores are not the best solution to be used.

8.4.3 Query by Data

If you need to search the keys based on something found in the value part of the key-value pairs, then key-value stores are not going to perform well for you. There is no way to inspect the value on the database side, with the exception of some products like Riak Search or indexing engines like Lucene [Lucene] or Solr [Solr].

8.4.4 Operations by Sets

Since operations are limited to one key at a time, there is no way to operate upon multiple keys at the same time. If you need to operate upon multiple keys, you have to handle this from the client side.

Chapter 9

Document Databases

Documents are the main concept in document databases. The database stores and retrieves documents, which can be XML, JSON, BSON, and so on. These documents are self-describing, hierarchical tree data structures which can consist of maps, collections, and scalar values. The documents stored are similar to each other but do not have to be exactly the same. Document databases store documents in the value part of the key-value store; think about document databases as key-value stores where the value is examinable. Let's look at how terminology compares in Oracle and MongoDB.

Oracle	MongoDB
database instance	MongoDB instance
schema	database
table	collection
row	document
rowid	_id
join	DBRef

The _id is a special field that is found on all documents in Mongo, just like ROWID in Oracle. In MongoDB, _id can be assigned by the user, as long as it is unique.

9.1 What Is a Document Database?

```
{ "firstname": "Martin",
  "likes": [ "Biking",
             "Photography" ],
  "lastcity": "Boston",
  "lastVisited":
}
```

The above document can be considered a row in a traditional RDBMS. Let's look at another document:

```
{
    "firstname": "Pramod",
    "citiesvisited": [ "Chicago", "London", "Pune", "Bangalore" ],
    "addresses": [
      { "state": "AK",
        "city": "DILLINGHAM",
        "type": "R"
      },
      { "state": "MH",
        "city": "PUNE",
        "type": "R" }
    ],
    "lastcity": "Chicago"
}
```

Looking at the documents, we can see that they are similar, but have differences in attribute names. This is allowed in document databases. The schema of the data can differ across documents, but these documents can still belong to the same collection—unlike an RDBMS where every row in a table has to follow the same schema. We represent a list of citiesvisited as an array, or a list of addresses as list of documents embedded inside the main document. Embedding child documents as subobjects inside documents provides for easy access and better performance.

If you look at the documents, you will see that some of the attributes are similar, such as firstname or city. At the same time, there are attributes in the second document which do not exist in the first document, such as addresses, while likes is in the first document but not the second.

This different representation of data is not the same as in RDBMS where every column has to be defined, and if it does not have data it is marked as empty or set to null. In documents, there are no empty attributes; if a given attribute is not found, we assume that it was not set or not relevant to the document. Documents allow for new attributes to be created without the need to define them or to change the existing documents.

Some of the popular document databases we have seen are MongoDB [MongoDB], CouchDB [CouchDB], Terrastore [Terrastore], OrientDB [OrientDB], RavenDB [RavenDB], and of course the well-known and often reviled Lotus Notes [Notes Storage Facility] that uses document storage.

9.2 Features

While there are many specialized document databases, we will use MongoDB as a representative of the feature set. Keep in mind that each product has some features that may not be found in other document databases.

Let's take some time to understand how MongoDB works. Each MongoDB instance has multiple *databases*, and each database can have multiple *collections*. When we compare this with RDBMS, an RDBMS instance is the same as MongoDB instance, the schemas in RDBMS are similar to MongoDB databases, and the RDBMS tables are collections in MongoDB. When we store a document, we have to choose which database and collection this document belongs in—for example, `database.collection.insert(document)`, which is usually represented as `db.coll.insert(document)`.

9.2.1 Consistency

Consistency in MongoDB database is configured by using the **replica sets** and choosing to wait for the writes to be replicated to all the slaves or a given number of slaves. Every write can specify the number of servers the write has to be propagated to before it returns as successful.

A command like `db.runCommand({ getlasterror : 1 , w : "majority" })` tells the database how strong is the consistency you want. For example, if you have one server and specify the w as `majority`, the write will return immediately since there is only one node. If you have three nodes in the replica set and specify w as `majority`, the write will have to complete at a minimum of two nodes before it is reported as a success. You can increase the w value for stronger consistency but you will suffer on write performance, since now the writes have to complete at more nodes. Replica sets also allow you to increase the read performance by allowing reading from slaves by setting `slaveOk`; this parameter can be set on the connection, or database, or collection, or individually for each operation.

```
Mongo mongo = new Mongo("localhost:27017");
mongo.slaveOk();
```

Here we are setting `slaveOk` per operation, so that we can decide which operations can work with data from the slave node.

```
DBCollection collection = getOrderCollection();
BasicDBObject query = new BasicDBObject();
query.put("name", "Martin");
DBCursor cursor = collection.find(query).slaveOk();
```

Similar to various options available for read, you can change the settings to achieve strong write consistency, if desired. By default, a write is reported successful once the database receives it; you can change this so as to wait for the writes to be synced to disk or to propagate to two or more slaves. This is known as WriteConcern: You make sure that certain writes are written to the master and some slaves by setting WriteConcern to REPLICAS_SAFE. Shown below is code where we are setting the WriteConcern for all writes to a collection:

```
DBCollection shopping = database.getCollection("shopping");
shopping.setWriteConcern(REPLICAS_SAFE);
```

WriteConcern can also be set per operation by specifying it on the save command:

```
WriteResult result = shopping.insert(order, REPLICAS_SAFE);
```

There is a tradeoff that you need to carefully think about, based on your application needs and business requirements, to decide what settings make sense for slaveOk during read or what safety level you desire during write with WriteConcern.

9.2.2 Transactions

Transactions, in the traditional RDBMS sense, mean that you can start modifying the database with insert, update, or delete commands over different tables and then decide if you want to keep the changes or not by using commit or rollback. These constructs are generally not available in NoSQL solutions—a write either succeeds or fails. Transactions at the single-document level are known as **atomic transactions**. Transactions involving more than one operation are not possible, although there are products such as RavenDB that do support transactions across multiple operations.

By default, all writes are reported as successful. A finer control over the write can be achieved by using WriteConcern parameter. We ensure that order is written to more than one node before it's reported successful by using WriteConcern.REPLICAS_SAFE. Different levels of WriteConcern let you choose the safety level during writes; for example, when writing log entries, you can use lowest level of safety, WriteConcern.NONE.

```
final Mongo mongo = new Mongo(mongoURI);
mongo.setWriteConcern(REPLICAS_SAFE);
DBCollection shopping = mongo.getDB(orderDatabase)
                        .getCollection(shoppingCollection);
```

```
try {
    WriteResult result = shopping.insert(order, REPLICAS_SAFE);
//Writes made it to primary and at least one secondary
} catch (MongoException writeException) {
//Writes did not make it to minimum of two nodes including primary
    dealWithWriteFailure(order, writeException);
}
```

9.2.3 Availability

The CAP theorem ("The CAP Theorem," p. 53) dictates that we can have only two of Consistency, Availability, and Partition Tolerance. Document databases try to improve on availability by replicating data using the master-slave setup. The same data is available on multiple nodes and the clients can get to the data even when the primary node is down. Usually, the application code does not have to determine if the primary node is available or not. MongoDB implements replication, providing high availability using **replica sets**.

In a replica set, there are two or more nodes participating in an asynchronous master-slave replication. The replica-set nodes elect the master, or primary, among themselves. Assuming all the nodes have equal voting rights, some nodes can be favored for being closer to the other servers, for having more RAM, and so on; users can affect this by assigning a priority—a number between 0 and 1000—to a node.

All requests go to the master node, and the data is replicated to the slave nodes. If the master node goes down, the remaining nodes in the replica set vote among themselves to elect a new master; all future requests are routed to the new master, and the slave nodes start getting data from the new master. When the node that failed comes back online, it joins in as a slave and catches up with the rest of the nodes by pulling all the data it needs to get current.

Figure 9.1 is an example configuration of replica sets. We have two nodes, **mongo A** and **mongo B**, running the MongoDB database in the primary datacenter, and **mongo C** in the secondary datacenter. If we want nodes in the primary datacenter to be elected as primary nodes, we can assign them a higher priority than the other nodes. More nodes can be added to the replica sets without having to take them offline.

The application writes or reads from the primary (master) node. When connection is established, the application only needs to connect to one node (primary or not, does not matter) in the replica set, and the rest of the nodes are discovered automatically. When the primary node goes down, the driver talks to the new primary elected by the replica set. The application does not have to manage any of the communication failures or node selection criteria. Using replica sets gives you the ability to have a highly available document data store.

Replica sets are generally used for data redundancy, automated failover, read scaling, server maintenance without downtime, and disaster recovery. Similar

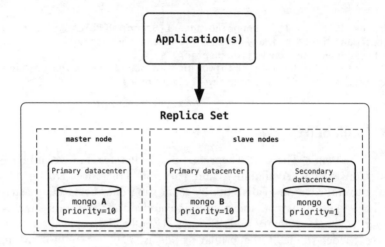

Figure 9.1 *Replica set configuration with higher priority assigned to nodes in the same datacenter*

availability setups can be achieved with CouchDB, RavenDB, Terrastore, and other products.

9.2.4 Query Features

Document databases provide different query features. CouchDB allows you to query via views—complex queries on documents which can be either materialized ("Materialized Views," p. 30) or dynamic (think of them as RDBMS views which are either materialized or not). With CouchDB, if you need to aggregate the number of reviews for a product as well as the average rating, you could add a view implemented via map-reduce ("Basic Map-Reduce," p. 68) to return the count of reviews and the average of their ratings.

When there are many requests, you don't want to compute the count and average for every request; instead you can add a materialized view that precomputes the values and stores the results in the database. These materialized views are updated when queried, if any data was changed since the last update.

One of the good features of document databases, as compared to key-value stores, is that we can query the data inside the document without having to retrieve the whole document by its key and then introspect the document. This feature brings these databases closer to the RDBMS query model.

MongoDB has a query language which is expressed via JSON and has constructs such as $query for the where clause, $orderby for sorting the data, or $explain to show the execution plan of the query. There are many more constructs like these that can be combined to create a MongoDB query.

Let's look at certain queries that we can do against MongoDB. Suppose we want to return all the documents in an order collection (all rows in the order table). The SQL for this would be:

```
SELECT * FROM order
```

The equivalent query in Mongo shell would be:

```
db.order.find()
```

Selecting the orders for a single `customerId` of `883c2c5b4e5b` would be:

```
SELECT * FROM order WHERE customerId = "883c2c5b4e5b"
```

The equivalent query in Mongo to get all orders for a single `customerId` of `883c2c5b4e5b`:

```
db.order.find({"customerId":"883c2c5b4e5b"})
```

Similarly, selecting `orderId` and `orderDate` for one customer in SQL would be:

```
SELECT orderId,orderDate FROM order WHERE customerId = "883c2c5b4e5b"
```

and the equivalent in Mongo would be:

```
db.order.find({customerId:"883c2c5b4e5b"},{orderId:1,orderDate:1})
```

Similarly, queries to count, sum, and so on are all available. Since the documents are aggregated objects, it is really easy to query for documents that have to be matched using the fields with child objects. Let's say we want to query for all the orders where one of the items ordered has a name like `Refactoring`. The SQL for this requirement would be:

```
SELECT * FROM customerOrder, orderItem, product
WHERE
customerOrder.orderId = orderItem.customerOrderId
AND orderItem.productId = product.productId
AND product.name LIKE '%Refactoring%'
```

and the equivalent Mongo query would be:

```
db.orders.find({"items.product.name":/Refactoring/})
```

The query for MongoDB is simpler because the objects are embedded inside a single document and you can query based on the embedded child documents.

9.2.5 Scaling

The idea of scaling is to add nodes or change data storage without simply migrating the database to a bigger box. We are not talking about making application changes to handle more load; instead, we are interested in what features are in the database so that it can handle more load.

Scaling for heavy-read loads can be achieved by adding more read slaves, so that all the reads can be directed to the slaves. Given a heavy-read application, with our 3-node replica-set cluster, we can add more read capacity to the cluster as the read load increases just by adding more slave nodes to the replica set to execute reads with the slaveOk flag (Figure 9.2). This is horizontal scaling for reads.

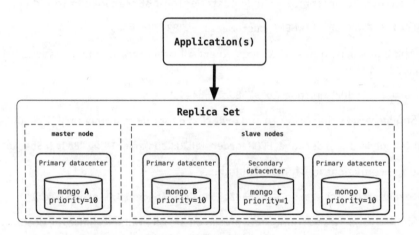

Figure 9.2   *Adding a new node, mongo D, to an existing replica-set cluster*

Once the new node, mongo D, is started, it needs to be added to the replica set.

```
rs.add("mongod:27017");
```

When a new node is added, it will sync up with the existing nodes, join the replica set as secondary node, and start serving read requests. An advantage of this setup is that we do not have to restart any other nodes, and there is no downtime for the application either.

When we want to scale for write, we can start sharding ("Sharding," p. 38) the data. Sharding is similar to partitions in RDBMS where we split data by value in a certain column, such as state or year. With RDBMS, partitions are usually on the same node, so the client application does not have to query a specific partition but can keep querying the base table; the RDBMS takes care of finding the right partition for the query and returns the data.

In sharding, the data is also split by certain field, but then moved to different Mongo nodes. The data is dynamically moved between nodes to ensure that shards are always balanced. We can add more nodes to the cluster and increase the number of writable nodes, enabling horizontal scaling for writes.

```
db.runCommand( { shardcollection : "ecommerce.customer",
                 key : {firstname : 1} } )
```

Splitting the data on the first name of the customer ensures that the data is balanced across the shards for optimal write performance; furthermore, each shard can be a replica set ensuring better read performance within the shard (Figure 9.3). When we add a new shard to this existing sharded cluster, the data will now be balanced across four shards instead of three. As all this data movement and infrastructure refactoring is happening, the application will not experience any downtime, although the cluster may not perform optimally when large amounts of data are being moved to rebalance the shards.

The shard key plays an important role. You may want to place your MongoDB database shards closer to their users, so sharding based on user location may be a good idea. When sharding by customer location, all user data for the East Coast of the USA is in the shards that are served from the East Coast, and all user data for the West Coast is in the shards that are on the West Coast.

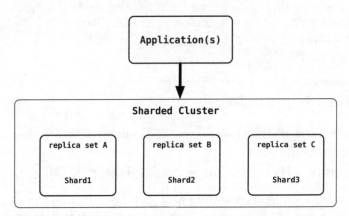

Figure 9.3 *MongoDB sharded setup where each shard is a replica set*

9.3 Suitable Use Cases

9.3.1 Event Logging

Applications have different event logging needs; within the enterprise, there are many different applications that want to log events. Document databases can store all these different types of events and can act as a central data store for event storage. This is especially true when the type of data being captured by the events keeps changing. Events can be sharded by the name of the application where the event originated or by the type of event such as order_processed or customer_logged.

9.3.2 Content Management Systems, Blogging Platforms

Since document databases have no predefined schemas and usually understand JSON documents, they work well in content management systems or applications for publishing websites, managing user comments, user registrations, profiles, web-facing documents.

9.3.3 Web Analytics or Real-Time Analytics

Document databases can store data for real-time analytics; since parts of the document can be updated, it's very easy to store page views or unique visitors, and new metrics can be easily added without schema changes.

9.3.4 E-Commerce Applications

E-commerce applications often need to have flexible schema for products and orders, as well as the ability to evolve their data models without expensive database refactoring or data migration ("Schema Changes in a NoSQL Data Store," p. 128).

9.4 When Not to Use

There are problem spaces where document databases are not the best solution.

9.4.1 Complex Transactions Spanning Different Operations

If you need to have atomic cross-document operations, then document databases may not be for you. However, there are some document databases that do support these kinds of operations, such as RavenDB.

9.4.2 Queries against Varying Aggregate Structure

Flexible schema means that the database does not enforce any restrictions on the schema. Data is saved in the form of application entities. If you need to query these entities ad hoc, your queries will be changing (in RDBMS terms, this would mean that as you join criteria between tables, the tables to join keep changing). Since the data is saved as an aggregate, if the design of the aggregate is constantly changing, you need to save the aggregates at the lowest level of granularity—basically, you need to normalize the data. In this scenario, document databases may not work.

Chapter 10

Column-Family Stores

Column-family stores, such as Cassandra [Cassandra], HBase [Hbase], Hypertable [Hypertable], and Amazon SimpleDB [Amazon SimpleDB], allow you to store data with keys mapped to values and the values grouped into multiple column families, each column family being a map of data.

RDBMS	Cassandra
database instance	cluster
database	keyspace
table	column family
row	row
column (same for all rows)	column (can be different per row)

10.1 What Is a Column-Family Data Store?

There are many column-family databases. In this chapter, we will talk about Cassandra but also reference other column-family databases to discuss features that may be of interest in particular scenarios.

Column-family databases store data in column families as rows that have many columns associated with a row key (Figure 10.1). Column families are groups of related data that is often accessed together. For a Customer, we would often access their Profile information at the same time, but not their Orders.

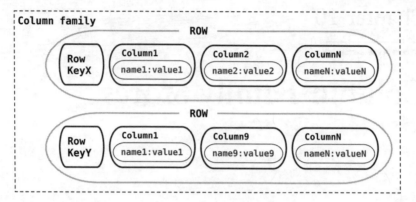

Figure 10.1 *Cassandra's data model with column families*

Cassandra is one of the popular column-family databases; there are others, such as HBase, Hypertable, and Amazon DynamoDB [Amazon DynamoDB]. Cassandra can be described as fast and easily scalable with write operations spread across the cluster. The cluster does not have a master node, so any read and write can be handled by any node in the cluster.

10.2 Features

Let's start by looking at how data is structured in Cassandra. The basic unit of storage in Cassandra is a column. A Cassandra column consists of a name-value pair where the name also behaves as the key. Each of these key-value pairs is a single column and is always stored with a timestamp value. The timestamp is used to expire data, resolve write conflicts, deal with stale data, and do other things. Once the column data is no longer used, the space can be reclaimed later during a compaction phase.

```
{
  name: "firstName",
  value: "Martin",
  timestamp: 12345667890
}
```

The column has a key of firstName and the value of Martin and has a time-stamp attached to it. A row is a collection of columns attached or linked to a key; a collection of similar rows makes a column family. When the columns in a column family are simple columns, the column family is known as **standard column family**.

```
//column family
{
//row
  "pramod-sadalage" : {
     firstName: "Pramod",
     lastName: "Sadalage",
     lastVisit: "2012/12/12"
  }
//row
  "martin-fowler" : {
     firstName: "Martin",
     lastName: "Fowler",
     location: "Boston"
  }
}
```

Each column family can be compared to a container of rows in an RDBMS table where the key identifies the row and the row consists of multiple columns. The difference is that various rows do not have to have the same columns, and columns can be added to any row at any time without having to add it to other rows. We have the pramod-sadalage row and the martin-fowler row with different columns; both rows are part of the column family.

When a column consists of a map of columns, then we have a **super column**. A super column consists of a name and a value which is a map of columns. Think of a super column as a container of columns.

```
{
  name: "book:978-0767905923",
  value: {
    author: "Mitch Albon",
    title: "Tuesdays with Morrie",
    isbn: "978-0767905923"
  }
}
```

When we use super columns to create a column family, we get a **super column family**.

```
//super column family
{
//row
name: "billing:martin-fowler",
value: {
  address: {
    name: "address:default",
    value: {
      fullName: "Martin Fowler",
      street:"100 N. Main Street",
      zip: "20145"
    }
  },
  billing: {
    name: "billing:default",
    value: {
      creditcard: "8888-8888-8888-8888",
      expDate: "12/2016"
      }
    }
  }
}
//row
name: "billing:pramod-sadalage",
value: {
  address: {
    name: "address:default",
    value: {
      fullName: "Pramod Sadalage",
      street:"100 E. State Parkway",
      zip: "54130"
    }
  },
  billing: {
    name: "billing:default",
    value: {
      creditcard: "9999-8888-7777-4444",
      expDate: "01/2016"
      }
    }
  }
}
```

Super column families are good to keep related data together, but when some of the columns are not needed most of the time, the columns are still fetched and deserialized by Cassandra, which may not be optimal.

Cassandra puts the standard and super column families into **keyspaces**. A keyspace is similar to a database in RDBMS where all column families related to the application are stored. Keyspaces have to be created so that column families can be assigned to them:

```
create keyspace ecommerce
```

10.2.1 Consistency

When a write is received by Cassandra, the data is first recorded in a commit log, then written to an in-memory structure known as **memtable**. A write operation is considered successful once it's written to the commit log and the memtable. Writes are batched in memory and periodically written out to structures known as **SSTable**. SSTables are not written to again after they are flushed; if there are changes to the data, a new SSTable is written. Unused SSTables are reclaimed by **compactation**.

Let's look at the read operation to see how consistency settings affect it. If we have a consistency setting of ONE as the default for all read operations, then when a read request is made, Cassandra returns the data from the first replica, even if the data is stale. If the data is stale, subsequent reads will get the latest (newest) data; this process is known as **read repair**. The low consistency level is good to use when you do not care if you get stale data and/or if you have high read performance requirements.

Similarly, if you are doing writes, Cassandra would write to one node's commit log and return a response to the client. The consistency of ONE is good if you have very high write performance requirements and also do not mind if some writes are lost, which may happen if the node goes down before the write is replicated to other nodes.

```
quorum = new ConfigurableConsistencyLevel();
quorum.setDefaultReadConsistencyLevel(HConsistencyLevel.QUORUM);
quorum.setDefaultWriteConsistencyLevel(HConsistencyLevel.QUORUM);
```

Using the QUORUM consistency setting for both read and write operations ensures that majority of the nodes respond to the read and the column with the newest timestamp is returned back to the client, while the replicas that do not have the newest data are repaired via the read repair operations. During write operations, the QUORUM consistency setting means that the write has to propagate to the majority of the nodes before it is considered successful and the client is notified.

Using ALL as consistency level means that all nodes will have to respond to reads or writes, which will make the cluster not tolerant to faults—even when one node is down, the write or read is blocked and reported as a failure. It's therefore upon the system designers to tune the consistency levels as the application requirements change. Within the same application, there may be different requirements of consistency; they can also change based on each operation, for example showing review comments for a product has different consistency requirements compared to reading the status of the last order placed by the customer.

During **keyspace** creation, we can configure how many replicas of the data we need to store. This number determines the replication factor of the data. If you have a replication factor of 3, the data copied on to three nodes. When writing and reading data with Cassandra, if you specify the consistency values of 2, you get that R + W is greater than the replication factor (2 + 2 > 3) which gives you better consistency during writes and reads.

We can run the node repair command for the keyspace and force Cassandra to compare every key it's responsible for with the rest of the replicas. As this operation is expensive, we can also just repair a specific column family or a list of column families:

```
repair ecommerce
```

```
repair ecommerce customerInfo
```

While a node is down, the data that was supposed to be stored by that node is handed off to other nodes. As the node comes back online, the changes made to the data are handed back to the node. This technique is known as **hinted handoff**. Hinted handoff allows for faster restore of failed nodes.

10.2.2 Transactions

Cassandra does not have transactions in the traditional sense—where we could start multiple writes and then decide if we want to commit the changes or not. In Cassandra, a write is atomic at the row level, which means inserting or updating columns for a given row key will be treated as a single write and will either succeed or fail. Writes are first written to commit logs and memtables, and are only considered good when the write to commit log and memtable was successful. If a node goes down, the commit log is used to apply changes to the node, just like the **redo log** in Oracle.

You can use external transaction libraries, such as ZooKeeper [ZooKeeper], to synchronize your writes and reads. There are also libraries such as Cages [Cages] that allow you to wrap your transactions over ZooKeeper.

10.2.3 Availability

Cassandra is by design highly available, since there is no master in the cluster and every node is a peer in the cluster. The availability of a cluster can be increased by reducing the consistency level of the requests. Availability is governed by the (R + W) > N formula ("Quorums," p. 57) where W is the minimum number of nodes where the write must be successfully written, R is the minimum number of nodes that must respond successfully to a read, and N is the number of nodes participating in the replication of data. You can tune the availability by changing the R and W values for a fixed value of N.

In a 10-node Cassandra cluster with a replication factor for the keyspace set to 3 (N = 3), if we set R = 2 and W = 2, then we have (2 + 2) > 3. In this scenario, when one node goes down, availability is not affected much, as the data can be retrieved from the other two nodes. If W = 2 and R = 1, when two nodes are down the cluster is not available for write but we can still read. Similarly, if

R = 2 and W = 1, we can write but the cluster is not available for read. With the R + W > N equation, you are making conscious decisions about consistency tradeoffs.

You should set up your keyspaces and read/write operations based on your needs—higher availability for write or higher availability for read.

10.2.4 Query Features

When designing the data model in Cassandra, it is advised to make the columns and column families optimized for reading the data, as it does not have a rich query language; as data is inserted in the column families, data in each row is sorted by column names. If we have a column that is retrieved much more often than other columns, it's better performance-wise to use that value for the row key instead.

10.2.4.1 *Basic Queries*

Basic queries that can be run using a Cassandra client include the GET, SET, and DEL. Before starting to query for data, we have to issue the keyspace command use ecommerce;. This ensures that all of our queries are run against the keyspace that we put our data into. Before starting to use the column family in the keyspace, we have to define the column family.

```
CREATE COLUMN FAMILY Customer
WITH comparator = UTF8Type
AND key_validation_class=UTF8Type
AND column_metadata = [
{column_name: city, validation_class: UTF8Type}
{column_name: name, validation_class: UTF8Type}
{column_name: web, validation_class: UTF8Type}
];
```

We have a column family named Customer with name, city, and web columns, and we are inserting data in the column family with a Cassandra client.

```
SET Customer['mfowler']['city']='Boston';
SET Customer['mfowler']['name']='Martin Fowler';
SET Customer['mfowler']['web']='www.martinfowler.com';
```

Using the Hector [Hector] Java client, we can insert the same data in the column family.

```
ColumnFamilyTemplate<String, String> template =
        cassandra.getColumnFamilyTemplate();
ColumnFamilyUpdater<String, String> updater =
        template.createUpdater(key);
for (String name : values.keySet()) {
    updater.setString(name, values.get(name));
}
```

```
try {
    template.update(updater);
} catch (HectorException e) {
    handleException(e);
}
```

We can read the data back using the GET command. There are multiple ways to get the data; we can get the whole column family.

```
GET Customer['mfowler'];
```

We can even get just the column we are interested in from the column family.

```
GET Customer['mfowler']['web'];
```

Getting the specific column we need is more efficient, as only the data we care about is returned—which saves lots of data movement, especially when the column family has a large number of columns. Updating the data is the same as using the SET command for the column that needs to be set to the new value. Using DEL command, we can delete either a column or the entire column family.

```
DEL Customer['mfowler']['city'];
```

```
DEL Customer['mfowler'];
```

10.2.4.2 *Advanced Queries and Indexing*

Cassandra allows you to index columns other than the keys for the column family. We can define an index on the city column.

```
UPDATE COLUMN FAMILY Customer
WITH comparator = UTF8Type
AND column_metadata = [{column_name: city,
                        validation_class: UTF8Type,
                        index_type: KEYS}];
```

We can now query directly against the indexed column.

```
GET Customer WHERE city = 'Boston';
```

These indexes are implemented as *bit-mapped* indexes and perform well for low-cardinality column values.

10.2.4.3 *Cassandra Query Language (CQL)*

Cassandra has a query language that supports SQL-like commands, known as Cassandra Query Language (CQL). We can use the CQL commands to create a column family.

```
CREATE COLUMNFAMILY Customer (
  KEY varchar PRIMARY KEY,
  name varchar,
  city varchar,
  web  varchar);
```

We insert the same data using CQL.

```
INSERT INTO Customer (KEY,name,city,web)
  VALUES ('mfowler',
          'Martin Fowler',
          'Boston',
          'www.martinfowler.com');
```

We can read data using the SELECT command. Here we read all the columns:

```
SELECT * FROM Customer
```

Or, we could just SELECT the columns we need.

```
SELECT name,web FROM Customer
```

Indexing columns are created using the CREATE INDEX command, and then can be used to query the data.

```
SELECT name,web FROM Customer WHERE city='Boston'
```

CQL has many more features for querying data, but it does not have all the features that SQL has. CQL does not allow joins or subqueries, and its where clauses are typically simple.

10.2.5 Scaling

Scaling an existing Cassandra cluster is a matter of adding more nodes. As no single node is a master, when we add nodes to the cluster we are improving the capacity of the cluster to support more writes and reads. This type of horizontal scaling allows you to have maximum uptime, as the cluster keeps serving requests from the clients while new nodes are being added to the cluster.

10.3 Suitable Use Cases

Let's discuss some of the problems where column-family databases are a good fit.

10.3.1 Event Logging

Column-family databases with their ability to store any data structures are a great choice to store event information, such as application state or errors encountered by the application. Within the enterprise, all applications can write their events to Cassandra with their own columns and the rowkey of the form `appname:timestamp`. Since we can scale writes, Cassandra would work ideally for an event logging system (Figure 10.2).

Figure 10.2 *Event logging with Cassandra*

10.3.2 Content Management Systems, Blogging Platforms

Using column families, you can store blog entries with tags, categories, links, and trackbacks in different columns. Comments can be either stored in the same row or moved to a different keyspace; similarly, blog users and the actual blogs can be put into different column families.

10.3.3 Counters

Often, in web applications you need to count and categorize visitors of a page to calculate analytics. You can use the `CounterColumnType` during creation of a column family.

```
CREATE COLUMN FAMILY visit_counter
WITH default_validation_class=CounterColumnType
AND key_validation_class=UTF8Type AND comparator=UTF8Type;
```

Once a column family is created, you can have arbitrary columns for each page visited within the web application for every user.

```
INCR visit_counter['mfowler'][home] BY 1;
INCR visit_counter['mfowler'][products] BY 1;
INCR visit_counter['mfowler'][contactus] BY 1;
```

Incrementing counters using CQL:

```
UPDATE visit_counter SET home = home + 1 WHERE KEY='mfowler'
```

10.3.4 Expiring Usage

You may provide demo access to users, or may want to show ad banners on a website for a specific time. You can do this by using **expiring columns**: Cassandra allows you to have columns which, after a given time, are deleted automatically. This time is known as TTL (Time To Live) and is defined in seconds. The column is deleted after the TTL has elapsed; when the column does not exist, the access can be revoked or the banner can be removed.

```
SET Customer['mfowler']['demo_access'] = 'allowed' WITH ttl=2592000;
```

10.4 When Not to Use

There are problems for which column-family databases are not the best solutions, such as systems that require ACID transactions for writes and reads. If you need the database to aggregate the data using queries (such as SUM or AVG), you have to do this on the client side using data retrieved by the client from all the rows.

Cassandra is not great for early prototypes or initial tech spikes: During the early stages, we are not sure how the query patterns may change, and as the query patterns change, we have to change the column family design. This causes friction for the product innovation team and slows down developer productivity. RDBMS impose high cost on schema change, which is traded off for a low cost of query change; in Cassandra, the cost may be higher for query change as compared to schema change.

Chapter 11

Graph Databases

Graph databases allow you to store entities and relationships between these entities. Entities are also known as nodes, which have properties. Think of a node as an instance of an object in the application. Relations are known as edges that can have properties. Edges have directional significance; nodes are organized by relationships which allow you to find interesting patterns between the nodes. The organization of the graph lets the data to be stored once and then interpreted in different ways based on relationships.

11.1 What Is a Graph Database?

In the example graph in Figure 11.1, we see a bunch of nodes related to each other. Nodes are entities that have properties, such as name. The node of Martin is actually a **node** that has **property** of name set to Martin.

We also see that edges have types, such as likes, author, and so on. These properties let us organize the nodes; for example, the nodes Martin and Pramod have an **edge** connecting them with a relationship type of friend. Edges can have multiple properties. We can assign a property of since on the friend relationship type between Martin and Pramod. Relationship types have directional significance; the friend relationship type is bidirectional but likes is not. When Dawn likes NoSQL Distilled, it does not automatically mean NoSQL Distilled likes Dawn.

Once we have a graph of these nodes and edges created, we can query the graph in many ways, such as "get all nodes employed by Big Co that like NoSQL Distilled." A query on the graph is also known as **traversing** the graph. An advantage of the graph databases is that we can change the traversing requirements without having to change the nodes or edges. If we want to "get all nodes that like NoSQL Distilled," we can do so without having to change the existing data or the model of the database, because we can traverse the graph any way we like.

111

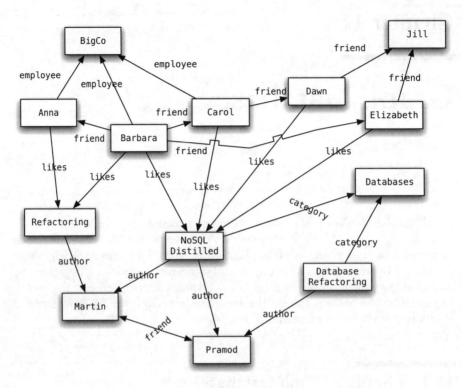

Figure 11.1   *An example graph structure*

Usually, when we store a graph-like structure in RDBMS, it's for a single type of relationship ("who is my manager" is a common example). Adding another relationship to the mix usually means a lot of schema changes and data movement, which is not the case when we are using graph databases. Similarly, in relational databases we model the graph beforehand based on the Traversal we want; if the Traversal changes, the data will have to change.

In graph databases, traversing the joins or relationships is very fast. The relationship between nodes is not calculated at query time but is actually persisted as a relationship. Traversing persisted relationships is faster than calculating them for every query.

Nodes can have different types of relationships between them, allowing you to both represent relationships between the domain entities and to have secondary relationships for things like category, path, time-trees, quad-trees for spatial indexing, or linked lists for sorted access. Since there is no limit to the number and kind of relationships a node can have, they can all be represented in the same graph database.

11.2 Features

There are many graph databases available, such as Neo4J [Neo4J], Infinite Graph [Infinite Graph], OrientDB [OrientDB], or FlockDB [FlockDB] (which is a special case: a graph database that only supports single-depth relationships or adjacency lists, where you cannot traverse more than one level deep for relationships). We will take Neo4J as a representative of the graph database solutions to discuss how they work and how they can be used to solve application problems.

In Neo4J, creating a graph is as simple as creating two nodes and then creating a relationship. Let's create two nodes, `Martin` and `Pramod`:

```
Node martin = graphDb.createNode();
martin.setProperty("name", "Martin");

Node pramod = graphDb.createNode();
pramod.setProperty("name", "Pramod");
```

We have assigned the `name` property of the two nodes the values of `Martin` and `Pramod`. Once we have more than one node, we can create a relationship:

```
martin.createRelationshipTo(pramod, FRIEND);
```

```
pramod.createRelationshipTo(martin, FRIEND);
```

We have to create relationship between the nodes in both directions, for the direction of the relationship matters: For example, a `product` node can be liked by `user` but the `product` cannot like the `user`. This directionality helps in designing a rich domain model (Figure 11.2). Nodes know about `INCOMING` and `OUTGOING` relationships that are traversable both ways.

Relationships are first-class citizens in graph databases; most of the value of graph databases is derived from the relationships. Relationships don't only have a type, a start node, and an end node, but can have properties of their own. Using these properties on the relationships, we can add intelligence to the relationship—for example, since when did they become friends, what is the distance between the nodes, or what aspects are shared between the nodes. These properties on the relationships can be used to query the graph.

Since most of the power from the graph databases comes from the relationships and their properties, a lot of thought and design work is needed to model the relationships in the domain that we are trying to work with. Adding new relationship types is easy; changing existing nodes and their relationships is similar to data migration ("Migrations in Graph Databases," p. 131), because these changes will have to be done on each node and each relationship in the existing data.

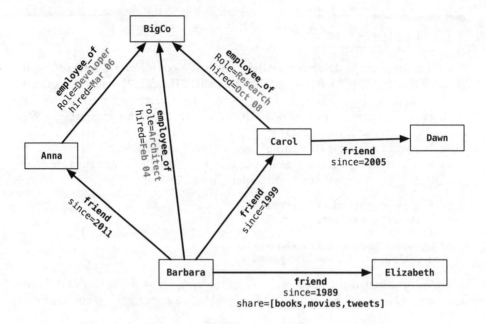

Figure 11.2   *Relationships with properties*

11.2.1 Consistency

Since graph databases are operating on connected nodes, most graph database solutions usually do not support distributing the nodes on different servers. There are some solutions, however, that support node distribution across a cluster of servers, such as Infinite Graph. Within a single server, data is always consistent, especially in Neo4J which is fully ACID-compliant. When running Neo4J in a cluster, a write to the master is eventually synchronized to the slaves, while slaves are always available for read. Writes to slaves are allowed and are immediately synchronized to the master; other slaves will not be synchronized immediately, though—they will have to wait for the data to propagate from the master.

Graph databases ensure consistency through transactions. They do not allow dangling relationships: The start node and end node always have to exist, and nodes can only be deleted if they don't have any relationships attached to them.

11.2.2 Transactions

Neo4J is ACID-compliant. Before changing any nodes or adding any relationships to existing nodes, we have to start a transaction. Without wrapping operations in transactions, we will get a `NotInTransactionException`. Read operations can be done without initiating a transaction.

```
Transaction transaction = database.beginTx();
try {
    Node node = database.createNode();
    node.setProperty("name", "NoSQL Distilled");
    node.setProperty("published", "2012");
    transaction.success();
} finally {
    transaction.finish();
}
```

In the above code, we started a transaction on the database, then created a node and set properties on it. We marked the transaction as success and finally completed it by finish. A transaction has to be marked as success, otherwise Neo4J assumes that it was a failure and rolls it back when finish is issued. Setting success without issuing finish also does not commit the data to the database. This way of managing transactions has to be remembered when developing, as it differs from the standard way of doing transactions in an RDBMS.

11.2.3 Availability

Neo4J, as of version 1.8, achieves high availability by providing for replicated slaves. These slaves can also handle writes: When they are written to, they synchronize the write to the current master, and the write is committed first at the master and then at the slave. Other slaves will eventually get the update. Other graph databases, such as Infinite Graph and FlockDB, provide for distributed storage of the nodes.

Neo4J uses the Apache ZooKeeper [ZooKeeper] to keep track of the last transaction IDs persisted on each slave node and the current master node. Once a server starts up, it communicates with ZooKeeper and finds out which server is the master. If the server is the first one to join the cluster, it becomes the master; when a master goes down, the cluster elects a master from the available nodes, thus providing high availability.

11.2.4 Query Features

Graph databases are supported by query languages such as Gremlin [Gremlin]. Gremlin is a domain-specific language for traversing graphs; it can traverse all graph databases that implement the Blueprints [Blueprints] property graph. Neo4J also has the Cypher [Cypher] query language for querying the graph. Outside these query languages, Neo4J allows you to query the graph for properties of the nodes, traverse the graph, or navigate the nodes relationships using language bindings.

Properties of a node can be indexed using the indexing service. Similarly, properties of relationships or edges can be indexed, so a node or edge can be found by the value. Indexes should be queried to find the starting node to begin a traversal. Let's look at searching for the node using node indexing.

If we have the graph shown in Figure 11.1, we can index the nodes as they are added to the database, or we can index all the nodes later by iterating over them. We first need to create an index for the nodes using the **IndexManager**.

```
Index<Node> nodeIndex = graphDb.index().forNodes("nodes");
```

We are indexing the nodes for the name property. Neo4J uses Lucene [Lucene] as its indexing service. We will see later that we can also use the full-text search capability of Lucene. When new nodes are created, they can be added to the index.

```
Transaction transaction = graphDb.beginTx();
try {
    Index<Node> nodeIndex = graphDb.index().forNodes("nodes");
    nodeIndex.add(martin, "name", martin.getProperty("name"));
    nodeIndex.add(pramod, "name", pramod.getProperty("name"));
    transaction.success();
} finally {
    transaction.finish();
}
```

Adding nodes to the index is done inside the context of a transaction. Once the nodes are indexed, we can search them using the indexed property. If we search for the node with the name of Barbara, we would query the index for the property of name to have a value of Barbara.

```
Node node = nodeIndex.get("name", "Barbara").getSingle();
```

We get the node whose name is Martin; given the node, we can get all its relationships.

```
Node martin = nodeIndex.get("name", "Martin").getSingle();
allRelationships = martin.getRelationships();
```

We can get both INCOMING or OUTGOING relationships.

```
incomingRelations = martin.getRelationships(Direction.INCOMING);
```

We can also apply directional filters on the queries when querying for a relationship. With the graph in Figure 11.1, if we want to find all people who like NoSQL Distilled, we can find the NoSQL Distilled node and then get its relationships with Direction.INCOMING. At this point we can also add the type of relationship to the query filter, since we are looking only for nodes that LIKE NoSQL Distilled.

```
Node nosqlDistilled = nodeIndex.get("name",
                          "NoSQL Distilled").getSingle();
relationships = nosqlDistilled.getRelationships(INCOMING, LIKES);
for (Relationship relationship : relationships) {
likesNoSQLDistilled.add(relationship.getStartNode());
}
```

Finding nodes and their immediate relations is easy, but this can also be achieved in RDBMS databases. Graph databases are really powerful when you want to traverse the graphs at any depth and specify a starting node for the traversal. This is especially useful when you are trying to find nodes that are related to the starting node at more than one level down. As the depth of the graph increases, it makes more sense to traverse the relationships by using a `Traverser` where you can specify that you are looking for `INCOMING`, `OUTGOING`, or `BOTH` types of relationships. You can also make the traverser go top-down or sideways on the graph by using `Order` values of `BREADTH_FIRST` or `DEPTH_FIRST`. The traversal has to start at some node—in this example, we try to find all the nodes at any depth that are related as a `FRIEND` with `Barbara`:

```
Node barbara = nodeIndex.get("name", "Barbara").getSingle();

Traverser friendsTraverser = barbara.traverse(Order.BREADTH_FIRST,
    StopEvaluator.END_OF_GRAPH,
    ReturnableEvaluator.ALL_BUT_START_NODE,
    EdgeType.FRIEND,
    Direction.OUTGOING);
```

The `friendsTraverser` provides us a way to find all the nodes that are related to `Barbara` where the relationship type is `FRIEND`. The nodes can be at any depth—friend of a friend at any level—allowing you to explore tree structures.

One of the good features of graph databases is finding paths between two nodes—determining if there are multiple paths, finding all of the paths or the shortest path. In the graph in Figure 11.1, we know that `Barbara` is connected to `Jill` by two distinct paths; to find all these paths and the distance between `Barbara` and `Jill` along those different paths, we can use

```
Node barbara = nodeIndex.get("name", "Barbara").getSingle();
Node jill = nodeIndex.get("name", "Jill").getSingle();
PathFinder<Path> finder = GraphAlgoFactory.allPaths(
        Traversal.expanderForTypes(FRIEND,Direction.OUTGOING)
                        ,MAX_DEPTH);
Iterable<Path> paths = finder.findAllPaths(barbara, jill);
```

This feature is used in social networks to show relationships between any two nodes. To find all the paths and the distance between the nodes for each path, we first get a list of distinct paths between the two nodes. The length of each path is the **number of hops** on the graph needed to reach the destination node from the start node. Often, you need to get the shortest path between two nodes; of the two paths from `Barbara` to `Jill`, the shortest path can be found by using

```
PathFinder<Path> finder = GraphAlgoFactory.shortestPath(
        Traversal.expanderForTypes(FRIEND, Direction.OUTGOING)
                        , MAX_DEPTH);
Iterable<Path> paths = finder.findAllPaths(barbara, jill);
```

Many other graph algorithms can be applied to the graph at hand, such as Dijkstra's algorithm [Dijkstra's] for finding the shortest or cheapest path between nodes.

```
START beginingNode = (beginning node specification)
MATCH (relationship, pattern matches)
WHERE (filtering condition: on data in nodes and relationships)
RETURN (What to return: nodes, relationships, properties)
ORDER BY (properties to order by)
SKIP (nodes to skip from top)
LIMIT (limit results)
```

Neo4J also provides the **Cypher** query language to query the graph. Cypher needs a node to START the query. The start node can be identified by its node ID, a list of node IDs, or index lookups. Cypher uses the MATCH keyword for matching patterns in relationships; the WHERE keyword filters the properties on a node or relationship. The RETURN keyword specifies what gets returned by the query—nodes, relationships, or fields on the nodes or relationships.

Cypher also provides methods to ORDER, AGGREGATE, SKIP, and LIMIT the data. In Figure 11.2, we find all nodes connected to Barbara, either incoming or outgoing, by using the --.

```
START barbara = node:nodeIndex(name = "Barbara")
MATCH (barbara)--(connected_node)
RETURN connected_node
```

When interested in directional significance, we can use

```
MATCH (barbara)<--(connected_node)
```

for incoming relationships or

```
MATCH (barbara)-->(connected_node)
```

for outgoing relationships. Match can also be done on specific relationships using the :RELATIONSHIP_TYPE convention and returning the required fields or nodes.

```
START barbara = node:nodeIndex(name = "Barbara")
MATCH (barbara)-[:FRIEND]->(friend_node)
RETURN friend_node.name,friend_node.location
```

We start with Barbara, find all outgoing relationships with the type of FRIEND, and return the friends' names. The relationship type query only works for the depth of one level; we can make it work for greater depths and find out the depth of each of the result nodes.

```
START barbara=node:nodeIndex(name = "Barbara")
MATCH path = barbara-[:FRIEND*1..3]->end_node
RETURN barbara.name,end_node.name, length(path)
```

Similarly, we can query for relationships where a particular relationship property exists. We can also filter on the properties of relationships and query if a property exists or not.

```
START barbara = node:nodeIndex(name = "Barbara")
MATCH (barbara)-[relation]->(related_node)
WHERE type(relation) = 'FRIEND' AND relation.share
RETURN related_node.name, relation.since
```

There are many other query features in the Cypher language that can be used to query database graphs.

11.2.5 Scaling

In NoSQL databases, one of the commonly used scaling techniques is sharding, where data is split and distributed across different servers. With graph databases, sharding is difficult, as graph databases are not aggregate-oriented but relationship-oriented. Since any given node can be related to any other node, storing related nodes on the same server is better for graph traversal. Traversing a graph when the nodes are on different machines is not good for performance. Knowing this limitation of the graph databases, we can still scale them using some common techniques described by Jim Webber [Webber Neo4J Scaling].

Generally speaking, there are three ways to scale graph databases. Since machines now can come with lots of RAM, we can add enough RAM to the server so that the working set of nodes and relationships is held entirely in memory. This technique is only helpful if the dataset that we are working with will fit in a realistic amount of RAM.

We can improve the read scaling of the database by adding more slaves with read-only access to the data, with all the writes going to the master. This pattern of writing once and reading from many servers is a proven technique in MySQL clusters and is really useful when the dataset is large enough to not fit in a single machine's RAM, but small enough to be replicated across multiple machines. Slaves can also contribute to availability and read-scaling, as they can be configured to never become a master, remaining always read-only.

When the dataset size makes replication impractical, we can shard (see the "Sharding" section on p. 38) the data from the application side using domain-specific knowledge. For example, nodes that relate to the North America can be created on one server while the nodes that relate to Asia on another. This application-level sharding needs to understand that nodes are stored on physically different databases (Figure 11.3).

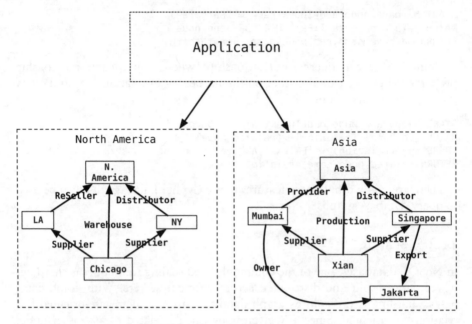

Figure 11.3   *Application-level sharding of nodes*

11.3 Suitable Use Cases

Let's look at some suitable use cases for graph databases.

11.3.1 Connected Data

Social networks are where graph databases can be deployed and used very effectively. These social graphs don't have to be only of the friend kind; for example, they can represent employees, their knowledge, and where they worked with other employees on different projects. Any link-rich domain is well suited for graph databases.

If you have relationships between domain entities from different domains (such as social, spatial, commerce) in a single database, you can make these relationships more valuable by providing the ability to traverse across domains.

11.3.2 Routing, Dispatch, and Location-Based Services

Every location or address that has a delivery is a node, and all the nodes where the delivery has to be made by the delivery person can be modeled as a graph of nodes. Relationships between nodes can have the property of distance, thus allowing you to deliver the goods in an efficient manner. Distance and location properties can also be used in graphs of places of interest, so that your application can provide recommendations of good restaurants or entertainment options nearby. You can also create nodes for your points of sales, such as bookstores or restaurants, and notify the users when they are close to any of the nodes to provide location-based services.

11.3.3 Recommendation Engines

As nodes and relationships are created in the system, they can be used to make recommendations like "your friends also bought this product" or "when invoicing this item, these other items are usually invoiced." Or, it can be used to make recommendations to travelers mentioning that when other visitors come to Barcelona they usually visit Antonio Gaudi's creations.

An interesting side effect of using the graph databases for recommendations is that as the data size grows, the number of nodes and relationships available to make the recommendations quickly increases. The same data can also be used to mine information—for example, which products are always bought together, or which items are always invoiced together; alerts can be raised when these conditions are not met. Like other recommendation engines, graph databases can be used to search for patterns in relationships to detect fraud in transactions.

11.4 When Not to Use

In some situations, graph databases may not be appropriate. When you want to update all or a subset of entities—for example, in an analytics solution where all entities may need to be updated with a changed property—graph databases may not be optimal since changing a property on all the nodes is not a straightforward operation. Even if the data model works for the problem domain, some databases may be unable to handle lots of data, especially in global graph operations (those involving the whole graph).

Chapter 12

Schema Migrations

12.1 Schema Changes

The recent trend in discussing NoSQL databases is to highlight their *schemaless* nature—it is a popular feature that allows developers to concentrate on the domain design without worrying about schema changes. It's especially true with the rise of agile methods [Agile Methods] where responding to changing requirements is important.

Discussions, iterations, and feedback loops involving domain experts and product owners are important to derive the right understanding of the data; these discussions must not be hampered by a database's schema complexity. With NoSQL data stores, changes to the schema can be made with the least amount of friction, improving developer productivity ("The Emergence of NoSQL," p. 9). We have seen that developing and maintaining an application in the brave new world of schemaless databases requires careful attention to be given to schema migration.

12.2 Schema Changes in RDBMS

While developing with standard RDBMS technologies, we develop objects, their corresponding tables, and their relationships. Consider a simple object model and data model that has `Customer`, `Order`, and `OrderItems`. The ER model would look like Figure 12.1.

While this data model supports the current object model, life is good. The first time there is a change in the object model, such as introducing `preferredShippingType` on the `Customer` object, we have to change the object and change the database table, because without changing the table the application will be out of sync with the database. When we get errors like `ORA-00942: table`

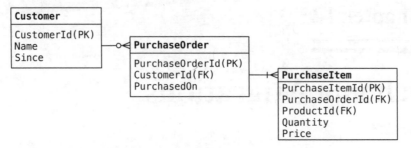

Figure 12.1 *Data model of an e-commerce system*

or view does not exist or ORA-00904: "PREFERRED_SHIPPING_TYPE": invalid identifier, we know we have this problem.

Typically, a database schema migration has been a project in itself. For deployment of the schema changes, database change scripts are developed, using diff techniques, for all the changes in the development database. This approach of creating migration scripts during the deployment/release time is error-prone and does not support agile development methods.

12.2.1 Migrations for Green Field Projects

Scripting the database schema changes during development is better, since we can store these schema changes along with the data migration scripts in the same script file. These script files should be named with incrementing sequential numbers which reflect the database versions; for example, the first change to the database could have script file named as 001_Description_Of_Change.sql. Scripting changes this way allows for the database migrations to be run preserving the order of changes. Shown in Figure 12.2 is a folder of all the changes done to a database so far.

Name ▲
📄 001_Customer.sql
📄 002_Product.sql
📄 003_Address.sql
📄 004_Order_OrderItem.sql
📄 005_Payment_Payment.sql
📄 006_Billing_Shipping.sql

Figure 12.2 *Sequence of migrations applied to a database*

Now, suppose we need to change the OrderItem table to store the DiscountedPrice and the FullPrice of the item. This will need a change to the OrderItem table and will be change number 007 in our sequence of changes, as shown in Figure 12.3.

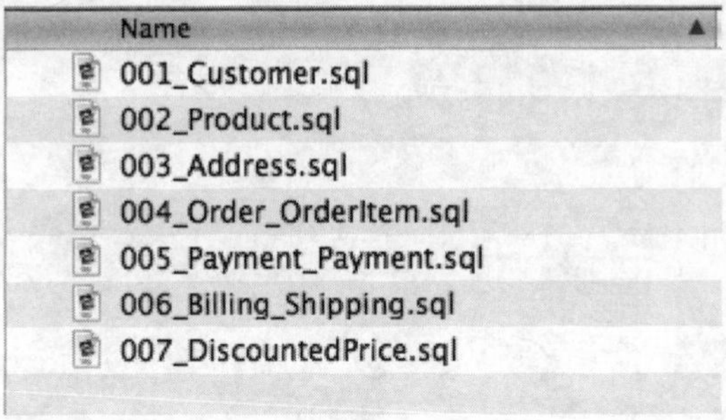

Name ▲
▤ 001_Customer.sql
▤ 002_Product.sql
▤ 003_Address.sql
▤ 004_Order_OrderItem.sql
▤ 005_Payment_Payment.sql
▤ 006_Billing_Shipping.sql
▤ 007_DiscountedPrice.sql

Figure 12.3 *New change* 007_DiscountedPrice.sql *applied to the database*

We applied a new change to the database. This change's script has the code for adding a new column, renaming the existing column, and migrating the data needed to make the new feature work. Shown below is the script contained in the change 007_DiscountedPrice.sql:

```
ALTER TABLE orderitem ADD discountedprice NUMBER(18,2) NULL;
UPDATE orderitem SET discountedprice = price;
ALTER TABLE orderitem MODIFY discountedprice NOT NULL;
ALTER TABLE orderitem RENAME COLUMN price TO fullprice;
--//@UNDO
ALTER TABLE orderitem RENAME fullprice TO price;
ALTER TABLE orderitem DROP COLUMN discountedprice;
```

The change script shows the schema changes to the database as well as the data migrations needed to be done. In the example shown, we are using DBDeploy [DBDeploy] as the framework to manage the changes to the database. DBDeploy maintains a table in the database, named ChangeLog, where all the changes made to the database are stored. In this table, Change_Number is what tells everyone which changes have been applied to the database. This Change_Number, which is the database version, is then used to find the corresponding numbered script in the folder and apply the changes which have not been applied yet. When we write a script with the change number 007 and apply it to the database using DBDeploy, DBDeploy will check the ChangeLog and pick up all the scripts from the folder that have not yet been applied. Figure 12.4 is the screenshot of DBDeploy applying the change to the database.

The best way to integrate with the rest of the developers is to use your project's version control repository to store all these change scripts, so that you can keep track of the version of the software and the database in the same place, eliminating

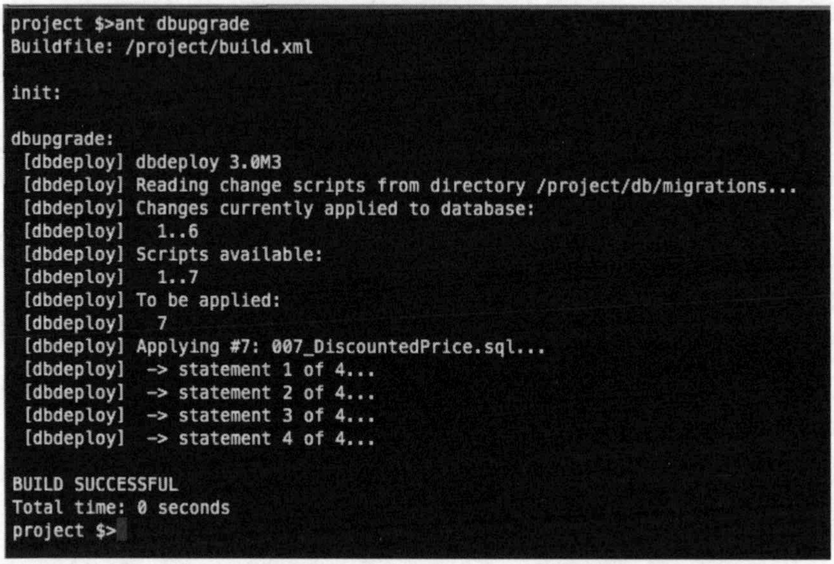

```
project $>ant dbupgrade
Buildfile: /project/build.xml

init:

dbupgrade:
  [dbdeploy] dbdeploy 3.0M3
  [dbdeploy] Reading change scripts from directory /project/db/migrations...
  [dbdeploy] Changes currently applied to database:
  [dbdeploy]   1..6
  [dbdeploy] Scripts available:
  [dbdeploy]   1..7
  [dbdeploy] To be applied:
  [dbdeploy]   7
  [dbdeploy] Applying #7: 007_DiscountedPrice.sql...
  [dbdeploy]   -> statement 1 of 4...
  [dbdeploy]   -> statement 2 of 4...
  [dbdeploy]   -> statement 3 of 4...
  [dbdeploy]   -> statement 4 of 4...

BUILD SUCCESSFUL
Total time: 0 seconds
project $>
```

Figure 12.4 *DBDeploy upgrading the database with change number 007*

possible mismatches between the database and the application. There are many other tools for such upgrades, including Liquibase [Liquibase], MyBatis Migrator [MyBatis Migrator], DBMaintain [DBMaintain].

12.2.2 Migrations in Legacy Projects

Not every project is a green field. How to implement migrations when an existing application is in production? We found that taking an existing database and extracting its structure into scripts, along with all the database code and any reference data, works as a baseline for the project. This baseline should not contain transactional data. Once the baseline is ready, further changes can be done using the migrations technique described above (Figure 12.5).

One of the main aspects of migrations should be maintaining backward compatibility of the database schema. In many enterprises there are multiple applications using the database; when we change the database for one application, this change should not break other applications. We can achieve backward compatibility by maintaining a transition phase for the change, as described in detail in *Refactoring Databases* [Ambler and Sadalage].

During a **transition phase**, the old schema and the new schema are maintained in parallel and are available for all the applications using the database. For this, we have to introduce scaffolding code, such as triggers, views, and virtual columns

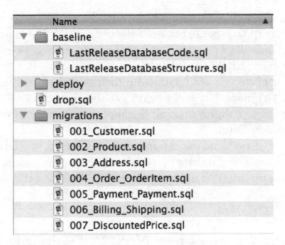

Figure 12.5   *Use of baseline scripts with a legacy database*

ensuring other applications can access the database schema and the data they require without any code changes.

```
ALTER TABLE customer ADD fullname VARCHAR2(60);
UPDATE customer SET fullname = fname;

CREATE OR REPLACE TRIGGER SyncCustomerFullName
BEFORE INSERT OR UPDATE
ON customer
REFERENCING OLD AS OLD NEW AS NEW
FOR EACH ROW
BEGIN
  IF :NEW.fname IS NULL THEN
    :NEW.fname := :NEW.fullname;
  END IF;
  IF :NEW.fullname IS NULL THEN
    :NEW.fullname := :NEW.fname
  END IF;
END;
/

--Drop Trigger and fname
--when all applications start using customer.fullname
```

In the example, we are trying to rename the customer.fname column to customer.fullname as we want to avoid any ambiguity of fname meaning either fullname or firstname. A direct rename of the fname column and changing the application code we are responsible for may just work, for our application—but will not for the other applications in the enterprise that are accessing the same database.

Using the transition phase technique, we introduce the new column `fullname`, copy the data over to `fullname`, but leave the old column `fname` around. We also introduce a `BEFORE UPDATE` trigger to synchronize data between the columns before they are committed to the database.

Now, when applications read data from the table, they will read either from `fname` or from `fullname` but will always get the right data. We can drop the trigger and the `fname` column once all the applications have moved on to using the new `fullname` column.

It's very hard to do schema migrations on large datasets in RDBMS, especially if we have to keep the database available to the applications, as large data movements and structural changes usually create locks on the database tables.

12.3 Schema Changes in a NoSQL Data Store

An RDBMS database has to be changed before the application is changed. This is what the *schema-free*, or *schemaless*, approach tries to avoid, aiming at flexibility of schema changes per entity. Frequent changes to the schema are needed to react to frequent market changes and product innovations.

When developing with NoSQL databases, in some cases the schema does not have to be thought about beforehand. We still have to design and think about other aspects, such as the types of relationships (with graph databases), or the names of the column families, rows, columns, order of columns (with column databases), or how are the keys assigned and what is the structure of the data inside the value object (with key-value stores). Even if we didn't think about these up front, or if we want to change our decisions, it is easy to do so.

The claim that NoSQL databases are entirely schemaless is misleading; while they store the data without regard to the schema the data adheres to, that schema has to be defined by the application, because the data stream has to be parsed by the application when reading the data from the database. Also, the application has to create the data that would be saved in the database. If the application cannot parse the data from the database, we have a schema mismatch even if, instead of the RDBMS database throwing a error, this error is now encountered by the application. Thus, even in schemaless databases, the schema of the data has to be taken into consideration when refactoring the application.

Schema changes especially matter when there is a deployed application and existing production data. For the sake of simplicity, assume we are using a document data store like MongoDB [MongoDB] and we have the same data model as before: `customer`, `order`, and `orderItems`.

```
{
"_id": "4BD8AE97C47016442AF4A580",
"customerid": 99999,
"name": "Foo Sushi Inc",
"since": "12/12/2012",
"order": {
    "orderid": "4821-UXWE-122012","orderdate": "12/12/2001",
    "orderItems": [{"product": "Fortune Cookies",
                    "price": 19.99}]
    }
}
```

Application code to write this document structure to MongoDB:

```
BasicDBObject orderItem = new BasicDBObject();
orderItem.put("product", productName);
orderItem.put("price", price);
orderItems.add(orderItem);
```

Code to read the document back from the database:

```
BasicDBObject item = (BasicDBObject) orderItem;
String productName = item.getString("product");
Double price = item.getDouble("price");
```

Changing the objects to add preferredShippingType does not require any change in the database, as the database does not care that different documents do not follow the same schema. This allows for faster development and easy deployments. All that needs to be deployed is the application—no changes on the database side are needed. The code has to make sure that documents that do not have the preferredShippingType attribute can still be parsed—and that's all.

Of course we are simplifying the schema change situation here. Let's look at the schema change we made before: introducing discountedPrice and renaming price to fullPrice. To make this change, we rename the price attribute to fullPrice and add discountedPrice attribute. The changed document is

```
{
"_id": "5BD8AE97C47016442AF4A580",
"customerid": 66778,
"name": "India House",
"since": "12/12/2012",
"order": {
  "orderid": "4821-UXWE-222012",
    "orderdate": "12/12/2001",
    "orderItems": [{"product": "Chair Covers",
                    "fullPrice": 29.99,
                    "discountedPrice":26.99}]
    }
}
```

Once we deploy this change, new customers and their orders can be saved and read back without problems, but for existing orders the price of their product cannot be read, because now the code is looking for fullPrice but the document has only price.

12.3.1 Incremental Migration

Schema mismatch trips many new converts to the NoSQL world. When schema is changed on the application, we have to make sure to convert all the existing data to the new schema (depending on data size, this might be an expensive operation). Another option would be to make sure that data, before the schema changed, can still be parsed by the new code, and when it's saved, it is saved back in the new schema. This technique, known as **incremental migration**, will migrate data over time; some data may never get migrated, because it was never accessed. We are reading both price and fullPrice from the document:

```
BasicDBObject item = (BasicDBObject) orderItem;
String productName = item.getString("product");
Double fullPrice = item.getDouble("price");
if (fullPrice == null) {
    fullPrice = item.getDouble("fullPrice");
}
Double discountedPrice = item.getDouble("discountedPrice");
```

When writing the document back, the old attribute price is not saved:

```
BasicDBObject orderItem = new BasicDBObject();
orderItem.put("product", productName);
orderItem.put("fullPrice", price);
orderItem.put("discountedPrice", discountedPrice);
orderItems.add(orderItem);
```

When using incremental migration, there could be many versions of the object on the application side that can translate the old schema to the new schema; while saving the object back, it is saved using the new object. This gradual migration of the data helps the application evolve faster.

The incremental migration technique will complicate the object design, especially as new changes are being introduced yet old changes are not being taken out. This period between the change deployment and the last object in the database migrating to the new schema is known as the transition period (Figure 12.6). Keep it as short as possible and focus it to the minimum possible scope—this will help you keep your objects clean.

The incremental migration technique can also be implemented with a schema_version field on the data, used by the application to choose the correct code to parse the data into the objects. When saving, the data is migrated to the latest version and the schema_version is updated to reflect that.

Having a proper translation layer between your domain and the database is important so that, as the schema changes, managing multiple versions of the

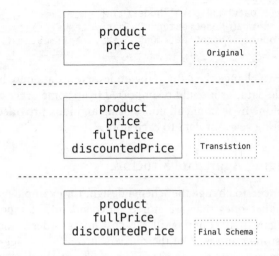

Figure 12.6 *Transition period of schema changes*

schema is restricted to the translation layer and does not leak into the whole application.

Mobile apps create special requirements. Since we cannot enforce the latest upgrades of the application, the application should be able to handle almost all versions of the schema.

12.3.2 Migrations in Graph Databases

Graph databases have edges that have types and properties. If you change the type of these edges in the codebase, you no longer can traverse the database, rendering it unusable. To get around this, you can traverse all the edges and change the type of each edge. This operation can be expensive and requires you to write code to migrate all the edges in the database.

If we need to maintain backward compatibility or do not want to change the whole graph in one go, we can just create new edges between the nodes; later when we are comfortable about the change, the old edges can be dropped. We can use traversals with multiple edge types to traverse the graph using the new and old edge types. This technique may help a great deal with large databases, especially if we want to maintain high availability.

If we have to change properties on all the nodes or edges, we have to fetch all the nodes and change all the properties that need to be changed. An example would be adding `NodeCreatedBy` and `NodeCreatedOn` to all existing nodes to track the changes being made to each node.

```
for (Node node : database.getAllNodes()) {
    node.setProperty("NodeCreatedBy", getSystemUser());
    node.setProperty("NodeCreatedOn", getSystemTimeStamp());
}
```

We may have to change the data in the nodes. New data may be derived from the existing node data, or it could be imported from some other source. The migration can be done by fetching all nodes using an index provided by the source of data and writing relevant data to each node.

12.3.3 Changing Aggregate Structure

Sometimes you need to change the schema design, for example by splitting large objects into smaller ones that are stored independently. Suppose you have a customer aggregate that contains all the customers orders, and you want to separate the customer and each of their orders into different aggregate units.

You then have to ensure that the code can work with both versions of the aggregates. If it does not find the old objects, it will look for the new aggregates.

Code that runs in the background can read one aggregate at a time, make the necessary change, and save the data back into different aggregates. The advantage of operating on one aggregate at a time is that this way, you're not affecting data availability for the application.

12.4 Further Reading

For more on migrations with relational databases, see [Ambler and Sadalage]. Although much of this content is specific to relational work, the general principles in migration will also apply to other databases.

12.5 Key Points

- Databases with strong schemas, such as relational databases, can be migrated by saving each schema change, plus its data migration, in a version-controlled sequence.

- Schemaless databases still need careful migration due to the implicit schema in any code that accesses the data.

- Schemaless databases can use the same migration techniques as databases with strong schemas.

- Schemaless databases can also read data in a way that's tolerant to changes in the data's implicit schema and use incremental migration to update data.

Chapter 13

Polyglot Persistence

Different databases are designed to solve different problems. Using a single database engine for all of the requirements usually leads to non- performant solutions; storing transactional data, caching session information, traversing graph of customers and the products their friends bought are essentially different problems. Even in the RDBMS space, the requirements of an OLAP and OLTP system are very different—nonetheless, they are often forced into the same schema.

Let's think of data relationships. RDBMS solutions are good at enforcing that relationships exist. If we want to discover relationships, or have to find data from different tables that belong to the same object, then the use of RDBMS starts being difficult.

Database engines are designed to perform certain operations on certain data structures and data amounts very well—such as operating on sets of data or a store and retrieving keys and their values really fast, or storing rich documents or complex graphs of information.

13.1 Disparate Data Storage Needs

Many enterprises tend to use the same database engine to store business transactions, session management data, and for other storage needs such as reporting, BI, data warehousing, or logging information (Figure 13.1).

The session, shopping cart, or order data do not need the same properties of availability, consistency, or backup requirements. Does session management storage need the same rigorous backup/recovery strategy as the e-commerce orders data? Does the session management storage need more availability of an instance of database engine to write/read session data?

In 2006, Neal Ford coined the term **polyglot programming**, to express the idea that applications should be written in a mix of languages to take advantage

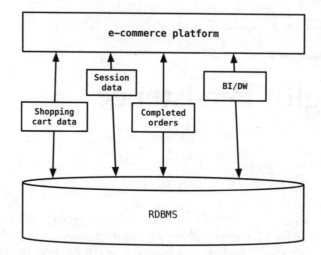

Figure 13.1 *Use of RDBMS for every aspect of storage for the application*

of the fact that different languages are suitable for tackling different problems. Complex applications combine different types of problems, so picking the right language for each job may be more productive than trying to fit all aspects into a single language.

Similarly, when working on an e-commerce business problem, using a data store for the shopping cart which is highly available and can scale is important, but the same data store cannot help you find products bought by the customers' friends—which is a totally different question. We use the term **polyglot persistence** to define this hybrid approach to persistence.

13.2 Polyglot Data Store Usage

Let's take our e-commerce example and use the polyglot persistence approach to see how some of these data stores can be applied (Figure 13.2). A key-value data store could be used to store the shopping cart data before the order is confirmed by the customer and also store the session data so that the RDBMS is not used for this transient data. Key-value stores make sense here since the shopping cart is usually accessed by user ID and, once confirmed and paid by the customer, can be saved in the RDBMS. Similarly, session data is keyed by the session ID.

If we need to recommend products to customers when they place products into their shopping carts—for example, "your friends also bought these products"

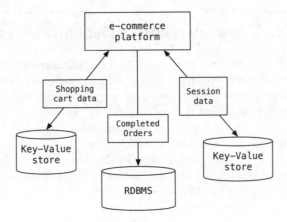

Figure 13.2 *Use of key-value stores to offload session and shopping cart data storage*

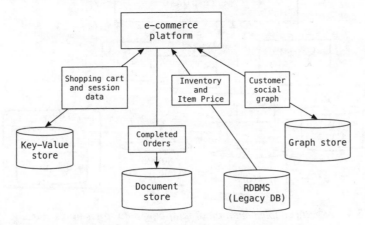

Figure 13.3 *Example implementation of polyglot persistence*

or "your friends bought these accessories for this product" — then introducing a graph data store in the mix becomes relevant (Figure 13.3).

It is not necessary for the application to use a single data store for all of its needs, since different databases are built for different purposes and not all problems can be elegantly solved by a singe database.

Even using specialized relational databases for different purposes, such as data warehousing appliances or analytics appliances within the same application, can be viewed as polyglot persistence.

13.3 Service Usage over Direct Data Store Usage

As we move towards multiple data stores in the application, there may be other applications in the enterprise that could benefit from the use of our data stores or the data stored in them. Using our example, the graph data store can serve data to other applications that need to understand, for example, which products are being bought by a certain segment of the customer base.

Instead of each application talking independently to the graph database, we can wrap the graph database into a service so that all relationships between the nodes can be saved in one place and queried by all the applications (Figure 13.4). The data ownership and the APIs provided by the service are more useful than a single application talking to multiple databases.

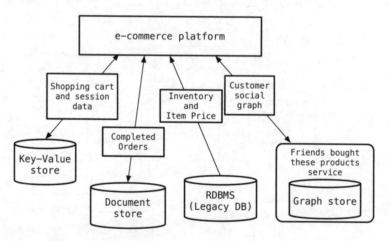

Figure 13.4 *Example implementation of wrapping data stores into services*

The philosophy of service wrapping can be taken further: You could wrap all databases into services, letting the application to only talk to a bunch of services (Figure 13.5). This allows for the databases inside the services to evolve without you having to change the dependent applications.

Many NoSQL data store products, such as Riak [Riak] and Neo4J [Neo4J], actually provide out-of-the-box REST API's.

13.4 Expanding for Better Functionality

Often, we cannot really change the data storage for a specific usage to something different, because of the existing legacy applications and their dependency on

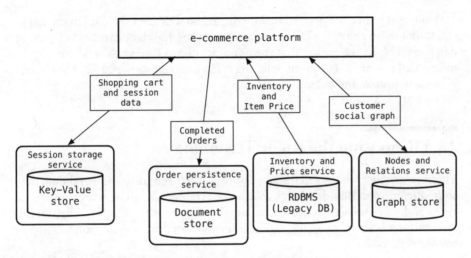

Figure 13.5 *Using services instead of talking to databases*

existing data storage. We can, however, add functionality such as caching for better performance, or use indexing engines such as Solr [Solr] so that search can be more efficient (Figure 13.6). When technologies like this are introduced, we have to make sure data is synchronized between the data storage for the application and the cache or indexing engine.

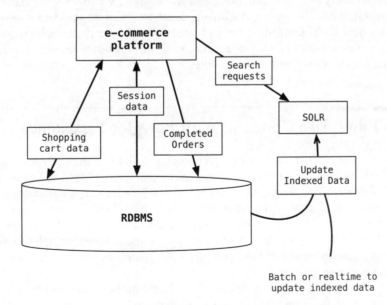

Figure 13.6 *Using supplemental storage to enhance legacy storage*

While doing this, we need to update the indexed data as the data in the application database changes. The process of updating the data can be real-time or batch, as long as we ensure that the application can deal with stale data in the index/search engine. The event sourcing ("Event Sourcing," p. 142) pattern can be used to update the index.

13.5 Choosing the Right Technology

There is a rich choice of data storage solutions. Initially, the pendulum had shifted from speciality databases to a single RDBMS database which allows all types of data models to be stored, although with some abstraction. The trend is now shifting back to using the data storage that supports the implementation of solutions natively.

If we want to recommend products to customers based on what's in their shopping carts and which other products were bought by customers who bought those products, it can be implemented in any of the data stores by persisting the data with the correct attributes to answer our questions. The trick is to use the right technology, so that when the questions change, they can still be asked with the same data store without losing existing data or changing it into new formats.

Let's go back to our new feature need. We can use RDBMS to solve this using a hierarchal query and modeling the tables accordingly. When we need to change the traversal, we will have to refactor the database, migrate the data, and start persisting new data. Instead, if we had used a data store that tracks relations between nodes, we could have just programmed the new relations and keep using the same data store with minimal changes.

13.6 Enterprise Concerns with Polyglot Persistence

Introduction of NoSQL data storage technologies will force the enterprise DBAs to think about how to use the new storage. The enterprise is used to having uniform RDBMS environments; whatever is the database an enterprise starts using first, chances are that over the years all its applications will be built around the same database. In this new world of polyglot persistence, the DBA groups will have to become more poly-skilled—to learn how some of these NoSQL technologies work, how to monitor these systems, back them up, and take data out of and put into these systems.

Once the enterprise decides to use any NoSQL technology, issues such as licensing, support, tools, upgrades, drivers, auditing, and security come up. Many

NoSQL technologies are open-source and have an active community of supporters; also, there are companies that provide commercial support. There is not a rich ecosystem of tools, but the tool vendors and the open-source community are catching up, releasing tools such as MongoDB Monitoring Service [Monitoring], Datastax Ops Center [OpsCenter], or Rekon browser for Riak [Rekon].

One other area that enterprises are concerned about is security of the data—the ability to create users and assign privileges to see or not see data at the database level. Most of the NoSQL databases do not have very robust security features, but that's because they are designed to operate differently. In traditional RDBMS, data was served by the database and we could get to the database using any query tools. With the NoSQL databases, there are query tools as well but the idea is for the application to own the data and serve it using services. With this approach, the responsibility for the security lies with the application. Having said that, there are NoSQL technologies that introduce security features.

Enterprises often have data warehouse systems, BI, and analytics systems that may need data from the polyglot data sources. Enterprises will have to ensure that the ETL tools or any other mechanism they are using to move data from source systems to the data warehouse can read data from the NoSQL data store. The ETL tool vendors are coming out with the ability to talk to NoSQL databases; for example, Pentaho [Pentaho] can talk to MongoDB and Cassandra.

Every enterprise runs analytics of some sort. As the sheer volume of data that needs to be captured increases, enterprises are struggling to scale their RDBMS systems to write all this data to the databases. A huge number of writes and the need to scale for writes are a great use case for NoSQL databases that allow you to write large volumes of data.

13.7 Deployment Complexity

Once we start down the path of using polyglot persistence in the application, **deployment complexity** needs careful consideration. The application now needs all databases in production at the same time. You will need to have these databases in your UAT, QA, and Dev environments. As most of the NoSQL products are open-source, there are few license cost ramifications. They also support automation of installation and configuration. For example, to install a database, all that needs to be done is download and unzip the archive, which can be automated using `curl` and `unzip` commands. These products also have sensible defaults and can be started with minimum configuration.

13.8 Key Points

- Polyglot persistence is about using different data storage technologies to handle varying data storage needs.

- Polyglot persistence can apply across an enterprise or within a single application.

- Encapsulating data access into services reduces the impact of data storage choices on other parts of a system.

- Adding more data storage technologies increases complexity in programming and operations, so the advantages of a good data storage fit need to be weighed against this complexity.

Chapter 14

Beyond NoSQL

The appearance of NoSQL databases has done a great deal to shake up and open up the world of databases, but we think the kind of NoSQL databases we have discussed here is only part of the picture of polyglot persistence. So it makes sense to spend some time discussing solutions that don't easily fit into the NoSQL bucket.

14.1 File Systems

Databases are very common, but file systems are almost ubiquitous. In the last couple of decades they've been widely used for personal productivity documents, but not for enterprise applications. They don't advertise any internal structure, so they are more like key-value stores with a hierarchic key. They also provide little control over concurrency other than simple file locking—which itself is similar to the way NoSQL only provides locking within a single aggregate.

File systems have the advantage of being simple and widely implemented. They cope well with very large entities, such as video and audio. Often, databases are used to index media assets stored in files. Files also work very well for sequential access, such as streaming, which can be handy for data which is append-only.

Recent attention to clustered environments has seen a rise of distributed file systems. Technologies like the Google File System and Hadoop [Hadoop] provide support for replication of files. Much of the discussion of map-reduce is about manipulating large files on cluster systems, with tools for automatic splitting of large files into segments to be processed on multiple nodes. Indeed a common entry path into NoSQL is from organizations that have been using Hadoop.

File systems work best for a relatively small number of large files that can be processed in big chunks, preferably in a streaming style. Large numbers of small files generally perform badly—this is where a data store becomes more efficient. Files also provide no support for queries without additional indexing tools such as Solr [Solr].

141

14.2 Event Sourcing

Event sourcing is an approach to persistence that concentrates on persisting all the changes to a persistent state, rather than persisting the current application state itself. It's an architectural pattern that works quite well with most persistence technologies, including relational databases. We mention it here because it also underpins some of the more unusual ways of thinking about persistence.

Consider an example of a system that keeps a log of the location of ships (Figure 14.1). It has a simple ship record that keeps the name of the ship and its current location. In the usual way of thinking, when we hear that the ship *King Roy* has arrived in San Francisco, we change the value of *King Roy*'s `location` field to `San Francisco`. Later on, we hear it's departed, so we change it to `at sea`, changing it again once we know it's arrived in Hong Kong.

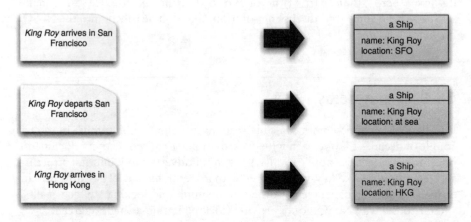

Figure 14.1 *In a typical system, notice of a change causes an update to the application's state.*

With an event-sourced system, the first step is to construct an event object that captures the information about the change (Figure 14.2). This event object is stored in a durable event log. Finally, we process the event in order to update the application's state.

As a consequence, in an event-sourced system we store every event that's caused a state change of the system in the event log, and the application's state is entirely derivable from this event log. At any time, we can safely throw away the application state and rebuild it from the event log.

In theory, event logs are all you need because you can always recreate the application state whenever you need it by replaying the event log. In practice, this may be too slow. As a result, it's usually best to provide the ability to store and recreate the application state in a snapshot. A **snapshot** is designed to persist the

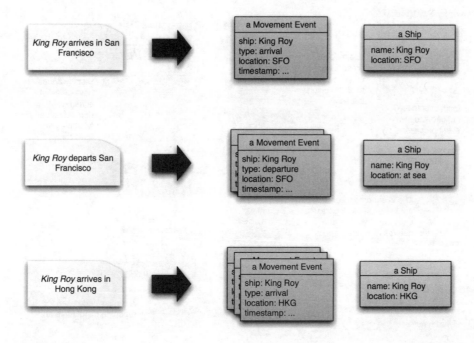

Figure 14.2 *With event sourcing, the system stores each event, together with the derived application state.*

memory image optimized for rapid recovery of the state. It is an optimization aid, so it should never take precedence over the event log for authority on the data.

How frequently you take a snapshot depends on your uptime needs. The snapshot doesn't need to be completely up to date, as you can rebuild memory by loading the latest snapshot and then replaying all events processed since that snapshot was taken. An example approach would be to take a snapshot every night; should the system go down during the day, you'd reload last night's snapshot followed by today's events. If you can do that quickly enough, all will be fine.

To get a full record of every change in your application state, you need to keep the event log going back to the beginning of time for your application. But in many cases such a long-lived record isn't necessary, as you can fold older events into a snapshot and only use the event log after the date of the snapshot.

Using event sourcing has a number of advantages. You can broadcast events to multiple systems, each of which can build a different application state for different purposes (Figure 14.3). For read-intensive systems, you can provide multiple read nodes, with potentially different schemas, while concentrating the writes on a different processing system (an approach broadly known as CQRS [CQRS]).

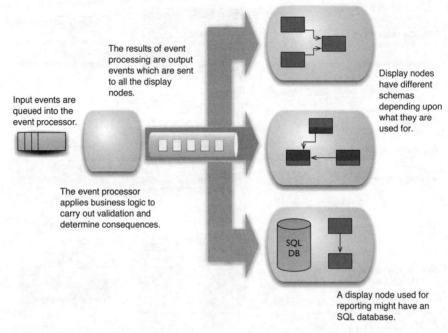

Figure 14.3 *Events can be broadcast to multiple display systems.*

Event sourcing is also an effective platform for analyzing historic information, since you can replicate any past state in the event log. You can also easily investigate alternative scenarios by introducing hypothetical events into an analysis processor.

Event sourcing does add some complexity—most notably, you have to ensure that all state changes are captured and stored as events. Some architectures and tools can make that inconvenient. Any collaboration with external systems needs to take the event sourcing into account; you'll need to be careful of external side effects when replaying events to rebuild an application state.

14.3 Memory Image

One of the consequences of event sourcing is that the event log becomes the definitive persistent record—but it is not necessary for the application state to be persistent. This opens up the option of keeping the application state in memory using only in-memory data structures. Keeping all your working data in memory provides a performance advantage, since there's no disk I/O to deal with when an event is processed. It also simplifies programming since there is no need to perform mapping between disk and in-memory data structures.

The obvious limitation here is that you must be able to store all the data you'll need to access in memory. This is an increasingly viable option—we can remember disk sizes that were considerably less than the current memory sizes. You also need to ensure that you can recover quickly enough from a system crash—either by reloading events from the event log or by running a duplicate system and cutting over.

You'll need some explicit mechanism to deal with concurrency. One route is a transactional memory system, such as the one that comes with the Clojure language. Another route is to do all input processing on a single thread. Designed carefully, a single-threaded event processor can achieve impressive throughput at low latency [Fowler lmax].

Breaking the separation between in-memory and persistent data also affects how you handle errors. A common approach is to update a model and roll back any changes should an error occur. With a memory image, you'll usually not have an automated rollback facility; you either have to write your own (complicated) or ensure that you do thorough validation before you begin to apply any changes.

14.4 Version Control

For most software developers, their most common experience of an event-sourced system is a version control system. Version control allows many people on a team to coordinate their modifications of a complex interconnected system, with the ability to explore past states of that system and alternative realities through branching.

When we think of data storage, we tend to think of a single-point-of-time worldview, which is very limiting compared to the complexity supported by a version control system. It's therefore surprising that data storage tools haven't borrowed some of the ideas from version control systems. After all, many situations require historic queries and support for multiple views of the world.

Version control systems are built on top of file systems, and thus have many of the same limitations for data storage as a file system. They are not designed for application data storage, so are awkward to use in that context. However, they are worth considering for scenarios where their timeline capabilities are useful.

14.5 XML Databases

Around the turn of the millennium, people seemed to want to use XML for everything, and there was a flurry of interest in databases specifically designed to store and query XML documents. While that flurry had as little impact on the relational dominance as previous blusters, XML databases are still around.

We think of XML databases as document databases where the documents are stored in a data model compatible with XML, and where various XML technologies are used to manipulate the document. You can use various forms of XML schema definitions (DTDs, XML Schema, RelaxNG) to check document formats, run queries with XPath and XQuery, and perform transformations with XSLT.

Relational databases took on XML and blended these XML capabilities with relational ones, usually by embedding XML documents as a column type and allowing some way to blend SQL and XML query languages.

Of course there's no reason why you can't use XML as a structuring mechanism within a key-value store. XML is less fashionable these days than JSON, but is equally capable of storing complex aggregates, and XML's schema and query capabilities are greater than what you can typically get for JSON. Using an XML database means that the database itself is able to take advantage of the XML structure and not just treat the value as a blob, but that advantage needs to be weighed with the other database characteristics.

14.6 Object Databases

When object-oriented programming started its rise in popularity, there was a flurry of interest in object-oriented databases. The focus here was the complexity of mapping from in-memory data structures to relational tables. The idea of an object-oriented database is that you avoid this complexity—the database would automatically manage the storage of in-memory structures onto disk. You could think of it as a persistent virtual memory system, allowing you to program with persistence yet without taking any notice of a database at all.

Object databases didn't take off. One reason was that the benefit of the close integration with the application meant you couldn't easily access data other than with that application. A shift from integration databases to application databases could well make object databases more viable in the future.

An important issue with object databases is how to deal with migration as the data structures change. Here, the close linkage between the persistent storage and in-memory structures can become a problem. Some object databases include the ability to add migration functions to object definitions.

14.7 Key Points

- NoSQL is just one set of data storage technologies. As they increase comfort with polyglot persistence, we should consider other data storage technologies whether or not they bear the NoSQL label.

Chapter 15

Choosing Your Database

At this point in the book, we've covered a lot of the general issues you need to be aware of to make decisions in the new world of polyglot persistence. It's now time to talk about choosing your databases for future development work. Naturally, we don't know your particular circumstances, so we can't give you your answer, nor can we reduce it to a simple set of rules to follow. Furthermore, it's still early days in the production use of NoSQL systems, so even what we do know is immature—in a couple of years we may well think differently.

We see two broad reasons to consider a NoSQL database: programmer productivity and data access performance. In different cases these forces may complement or contradict each other. Both of them are difficult to assess early on in a project, which is awkward since your choice of a data storage model is difficult to abstract so as to allow you to change your mind later on.

15.1 Programmer Productivity

Talk to any developer of an enterprise application, and you'll sense frustration from working with relational databases. Information is usually collected and displayed in terms of aggregates, but it has to be transformed into relations in order to persist it. This chore is easier than it used to be; during the 1990s many projects groaned under the effort of building object-relational mapping layers. By the 2000s, we've seen popular ORM frameworks such as Hibernate, iBATIS, and Rails Active Record that reduce much of that burden. But this has not made the problem go away. ORMs are a leaky abstraction, there are always some cases that need more attention—particularly in order to get decent performance.

In this situation aggregate-oriented databases can offer a tempting deal. We can remove the ORM and persist aggregates naturally as we use them. We've come across several projects that claim palpable benefits from moving to an aggregate-oriented solution.

Graph databases offer a different simplification. Relational databases do not do a good job with data that has a lot of relationships. A graph database offers both a more natural storage API for this kind of data and query capabilities designed around these kinds of structures.

All kinds of NoSQL systems are better suited to nonuniform data. If you find yourself struggling with a strong schema in order to support ad-hoc fields, then the schemaless NoSQL databases can offer considerable relief.

These are the major reasons why the programming model of NoSQL databases may improve the productivity of your development team. The first step of assessing this for your circumstances is to look at what your software will need to do. Run through the current features and see if and how the data usage fits. As you do this, you may begin to see that a particular data model seems like a good fit. That closeness of fit suggests that using that model will lead to easier programming.

As you do this, remember that polyglot persistence is about using multiple data storage solutions. It may be that you'll see different data storage models fit different parts of your data. This would suggest using different databases for different aspects of your data. Using multiple databases is inherently more complex than using a single store, but the advantages of a good fit in each case may be better overall.

As you look at the data model fit, pay particular attention to cases where there is a problem. You may see most of your features will work well with an aggregate, but a few will not. Having a few features that don't fit the model well isn't a reason to avoid the model—the difficulties of the bad fit may not overwhelm the advantages of the good fit—but it's useful to spot and highlight these bad fit cases.

Going through your features and assessing your data needs should lead you to one or more alternatives for how to handle your database needs. This will give you a starting point, but the next step is to try things out by actually building software. Take some initial features and build them, while paying close attention to how straightforward it is to use the technology you're considering. In this situation, it may be worthwhile to build the same features with a couple of different databases in order to see which works best. People are often reluctant to do this—no one likes to build software that will be discarded. Yet this is an essential way to judge how effective a particular framework is.

Sadly, there is no way to properly measure how productive different designs are. We have no way of properly measuring output. Even if you build exactly the same feature, you can't truly compare the productivity because knowledge of building it once makes it easier a second time, and you can't build them simultaneously with identical teams. What you can do is ensure the people who did the work can give an opinion. Most developers can sense when they are more productive in one environment than another. Although this is a subjective judgment, and you may well get disagreements between team members, this is the best judgment you will get. In the end we believe the team doing the work should decide.

When trying out a database to judge productivity, it's important to also try out some of the bad fit cases we mentioned earlier. That way the team can get a feeling of both the happy path and the difficult one, to gain an overall impression.

This approach has its flaws. Often you can't get a full appreciation of a technology without spending many months using it—and running an assessment for that long is rarely cost-effective. But like many things in life, we need to make the best assessment we can, knowing its flaws, and go with that. The essential thing here is to base the decision on as much real programming as you can. Even a mere week working with a technology can tell you things you'd never learn from a hundred vendor presentations.

15.2 Data-Access Performance

The concern that led to the growth of NoSQL databases was rapid access to lots of data. As large websites emerged, they wanted to grow horizontally and run on large clusters. They developed the early NoSQL databases to help them run efficiently on such architectures. As other data users follow their lead, again the focus is on accessing data rapidly, often with large volumes involved.

There are many factors that can determine a database's better performance than the relational default in various circumstances. An aggregate-oriented database may be very fast for reading or retrieving aggregates compared to a relational database where data is spread over many tables. Easier sharding and replication over clusters allows horizontal scaling. A graph database can retrieve highly connected data more quickly than using relational joins.

If you're investigating NoSQL databases based on performance, the most important thing you must do is to test their performance in the scenarios that matter to you. Reasoning about how a database may perform can help you build a short list, but the only way you can assess performance properly is to build something, run it, and measure it.

When building a performance assessment, the hardest thing is often getting a realistic set of performance tests. You can't build your actual system, so you need to build a representative subset. It's important, however, for this subset to be as faithful a representative as possible. It's no good taking a database that's intended to serve hundreds of concurrent users and assessing its performance with a single user. You are going to need to build representative loads and data volumes.

Particularly if you are building a public website, it can be difficult to build a high-load testbed. Here, a good argument can be made for using cloud computing resources both to generate load and to build a test cluster. The elastic nature of cloud provisioning is very helpful for short-lived performance assessment work.

You're not going to be able to test every way in which your application will be used, so you need to build a representative subset. Choose scenarios that are the most common, the most performance-dependent, and those that don't seem to fit your database model well. The latter may alert you to any risks outside of your main use cases.

Coming up with volumes to test for can be tricky, especially early on in a project when it's not clear what your production volumes are likely to be. You will have to come up with something to base your thinking on, so be sure to make it explicit and to communicate it with all the stakeholders. Making it explicit reduces the chance that different people have varying ideas on what a "heavy read load" is. It also allows you to spot problems more easily should your later discoveries wander off your original assumptions. Without making your assumptions explicit, it's easier to drift away from them without realizing you need to redo your testbed as you learn new information.

15.3 Sticking with the Default

Naturally we think that NoSQL is a viable option in many circumstances—otherwise we wouldn't have spent several months writing this book. But we also realize that there are many cases, indeed the majority of cases, where you're better off sticking with the default option of a relational database.

Relational databases are well known; you can easily find people with the experience of using them. They are mature, so you are less likely to run into the rough edges of new technology. There are lots of tools that are built on relational technology that you can take advantage of. You also don't have to deal with the political issues of making an unusual choice—picking a new technology will always introduce a risk of problems should things run into difficulties.

So, on the whole, we tend to take a view that to choose a NoSQL database you need to show a real advantage over relational databases for your situation. There's no shame in doing the assessments for programmability and performance, finding no clear advantage, and staying with the relational option. We think there are many cases where it is advantageous to use NoSQL databases, but "many" does not mean "all" or even "most."

15.4 Hedging Your Bets

One of the greatest difficulties we have in giving advice on choosing a data-storage option is that we don't have that much data to go on. As we write this, we are only seeing very early adopters discussing their experiences with these technologies, so we don't have a clear picture of the actual pros and cons.

With the situation this uncertain, there's more of an argument for encapsulating your database choice—keeping all your database code in a section of your codebase that is relatively easy to replace should you decide to change your database choice later. The classic way to do this is through an explicit data store layer in your application—using patterns such as Data Mapper and Repository [Fowler PoEAA]. Such an encapsulation layer does carry a cost, particularly when you are unsure about using quite different models, such as key-value versus graph data models. Worse still, we don't have experience yet with encapsulating data layers between these very different kinds of data stores.

On the whole, our advice is to encapsulate as a default strategy, but pay attention to the cost of insulating layer. If it's getting too much of a burden, for example by making it harder to use some helpful database features, then it's a good argument for using the database that has those features. This information may be just what you need to make a database choice and thus eliminate the encapsulation.

This is another argument for decomposing the database layer into services that encapsulate data storage ("Service Usage over Direct Data Store Usage," p. 136). As well as reducing coupling between various services, this has the additional advantage of making it easier to replace a database should things not work out in the future. This is a plausible approach even if you end up using the same database everywhere—should things go badly, you can gradually swap it out, focusing on the most problematic services first.

This design advice applies just as much if you prefer to stick with a relational option. By encapsulating segments of your database into services, you can replace parts of your data store with a NoSQL technology as it matures and the advantages become clearer.

15.5 Key Points

- The two main reasons to use NoSQL technology are:

    - To improve programmer productivity by using a database that better matches an application's needs.

    - To improve data access performance via some combination of handling larger data volumes, reducing latency, and improving throughput.

- It's essential to test your expectations about programmer productivity and/or performance before committing to using a NoSQL technology.

- Service encapsulation supports changing data storage technologies as needs and technology evolve. Separating parts of applications into services also allows you to introduce NoSQL into an existing application.

- Most applications, particularly nonstrategic ones, should stick with relational technology—at least until the NoSQL ecosystem becomes more mature.

15.6 Final Thoughts

We hope you've found this book enlightening. When we started writing it, we were frustrated by the lack of anything that would give us a broad survey of the NoSQL world. In writing this book we had to make that survey ourselves, and we've found it an enjoyable journey. We hope your journey through this material is considerably quicker but no less enjoyable.

At this point you may be considering making use of a NoSQL technology. If so this book is only an early step in building your understanding. We urge you to download some databases and work with them, for we're of the firm conviction that you can only understand a technology properly by working with it—finding its strengths and the inevitable gotchas that never make it into the documentation.

We expect that most people, including most readers of this book, will not be using NoSQL for a while. It is a new technology and we are still early in the process of understanding when to use it and how to use it well. But as with anything in the software world, things are changing more rapidly than we dare predict, so do keep an eye on what's happening in this field.

We hope you'll also find other books and articles to help you. We think the best material on NoSQL will be written after this book is done, so we can't point you to anywhere in particular as we write this. We do have an active presence on the Web, so for our more up-to-date thoughts on the NoSQL world take a look at www.sadalage.com and http://martinfowler.com/nosql.html.

Bibliography

[Agile Methods] www.agilealliance.org.

[Amazon's Dynamo] www.allthingsdistributed.com/2007/10/amazons_dynamo.html.

[Amazon DynamoDB] http://aws.amazon.com/dynamodb.

[Amazon SimpleDB] http://aws.amazon.com/simpledb.

[Ambler and Sadalage] Ambler, Scott and Pramodkumar Sadalage. *Refactoring Databases: Evolutionary Database Design*. Addison-Wesley. 2006. ISBN 978-0321293534.

[Berkeley DB] www.oracle.com/us/products/database/berkeley-db.

[Blueprints] https://github.com/tinkerpop/blueprints/wiki.

[Brewer] Brewer, Eric. *Towards Robust Distributed Systems*. www.cs.berkeley.edu/~brewer/cs262b-2004/PODC-keynote.pdf.

[Cages] http://code.google.com/p/cages.

[Cassandra] http://cassandra.apache.org.

[Chang etc.] Chang, Fay, Jeffrey Dean, Sanjay Ghemawat, Wilson C. Hsieh, Deborah A. Wallach, Mike Burrows, Tushar Chandra, Andrew Fikes, and Robert E. Gruber. *Bigtable: A Distributed Storage System for Structured Data*. http://research.google.com/archive/bigtable-osdi06.pdf.

[CouchDB] http://couchdb.apache.org.

[CQL] www.slideshare.net/jericevans/cql-sql-in-cassandra.

[CQRS] http://martinfowler.com/bliki/CQRS.html.

[C-Store] Stonebraker, Mike, Daniel Abadi, Adam Batkin, Xuedong Chen, Mitch Cherniack, Miguel Ferreira, Edmond Lau, Amerson Lin, Sam Madden, Elizabeth O'Neil, Pat O'Neil, Alex Rasin, Nga Tran, and Stan Zdonik. *C-Store: A Column-oriented DBMS*. http://db.csail.mit.edu/projects/cstore/vldb.pdf.

[Cypher] http://docs.neo4j.org/chunked/1.6.1/cypher-query-lang.html.

[Daigneau] Daigneau, Robert. *Service Design Patterns*. Addison-Wesley. 2012. ISBN 032154420X.

[DBDeploy] http://dbdeploy.com.

[DBMaintain] www.dbmaintain.org.

[Dean and Ghemawat] Dean, Jeffrey and Sanjay Ghemawat. *MapReduce: Simplified Data Processing on Large Clusters.* http://static.usenix.org/event/osdi04/tech/full_papers/dean/dean.pdf.

[Dijkstra's] http://en.wikipedia.org/wiki/Dijkstra%27s_algorithm.

[Evans] Evans, Eric. *Domain-Driven Design.* Addison-Wesley. 2004. ISBN 0321125215.

[FlockDB] https://github.com/twitter/flockdb.

[Fowler DSL] Fowler, Martin. *Domain-Specific Languages.* Addison-Wesley. 2010. ISBN 0321712943.

[Fowler lmax] Fowler, Martin. *The LMAX Architecture.* http://martinfowler.com/articles/lmax.html.

[Fowler PoEAA] Fowler, Martin. *Patterns of Enterprise Application Architecture.* Addison-Wesley. 2003. ISBN 0321127420.

[Fowler UML] Fowler, Martin. *UML Distilled.* Addison-Wesley. 2003. ISBN 0321193687.

[Gremlin] https://github.com/tinkerpop/gremlin/wiki.

[Hadoop] http://hadoop.apache.org/mapreduce.

[HamsterDB] http://hamsterdb.com.

[Hbase] http://hbase.apache.org.

[Hector] https://github.com/rantav/hector.

[Hive] http://hive.apache.org.

[Hohpe and Woolf] Hohpe, Gregor and Bobby Woolf. *Enterprise Integration Patterns.* Addison-Wesley. 2003. ISBN 0321200683.

[HTTP] Fielding, R., J. Gettys, J. Mogul, H. Frystyk, L. Masinter, P. Leach, and T. Berners-Lee. *Hypertext Transfer Protocol—HTTP/1.1.* www.w3.org/Protocols/rfc2616/rfc2616.html.

[Hypertable] http://hypertable.org.

[Infinite Graph] www.infinitegraph.com.

[JSON] http://json.org.

[LevelDB] http://code.google.com/p/leveldb.

[Liquibase] www.liquibase.org.

[Lucene] http://lucene.apache.org.

[Lynch and Gilbert] Lynch, Nancy and Seth Gilbert. *Brewer's conjecture and the feasibility of consistent, available, partition-tolerant web services.* http://lpd.epfl.ch/sgilbert/pubs/BrewersConjecture-SigAct.pdf.

[Memcached] http://memcached.org.

[MongoDB] www.mongodb.org.

[Monitoring] www.mongodb.org/display/DOCS/MongoDB+Monitoring+Service.

[MyBatis Migrator] http://mybatis.org.

[Neo4J] http://neo4j.org.

[NoSQL Debrief] http://blog.oskarsson.nu/post/22996140866/nosql-debrief.

[NoSQL Meetup] http://nosql.eventbrite.com.

[Notes Storage Facility] http://en.wikipedia.org/wiki/IBM_Lotus_Domino.

[OpsCenter] www.datastax.com/products/opscenter.

[OrientDB] www.orientdb.org.

[Oskarsson] *Private Correspondence.*

[Pentaho] www.pentaho.com.

[Pig] http://pig.apache.org.

[Pritchett] www.infoq.com/interviews/dan-pritchett-ebay-architecture.

[Project Voldemort] http://project-voldemort.com.

[RavenDB] http://ravendb.net.

[Redis] http://redis.io.

[Rekon] https://github.com/basho/rekon.

[Riak] http://wiki.basho.com/Riak.html.

[Solr] http://lucene.apache.org/solr.

[Strozzi NoSQL] www.strozzi.it/cgi-bin/CSA/tw7/I/en_US/NoSQL.

[Tanenbaum and Van Steen] Tanenbaum, Andrew and Maarten Van Steen. *Distributed Systems.* Prentice-Hall. 2007. ISBN 0132392275.

[Terrastore] http://code.google.com/p/terrastore.

[Vogels] Vogels, Werner. *Eventually Consistent—Revisited.* www.allthingsdistributed.com/2008/12/eventually_consistent.html.

[Webber Neo4J Scaling] http://jim.webber.name/2011/03/22/ef4748c3-6459-40b6-bcfa-818960150e0f.aspx.

[ZooKeeper] http://zookeeper.apache.org.

Index

A

ACID (Atomic, Consistent, Isolated, and Durable) transactions, 19
  in column-family databases, 109
  in graph databases, 28, 50, 114–115
  in relational databases, 10, 26
  vs. BASE, 56
ad banners, 108–109
aggregate-oriented databases, 14, 19–23, 147
  atomic updates in, 50, 61
  disadvantages of, 30
  no ACID transactions in, 50
  performance of, 149
  vs. graph databases, 28
aggregates, 14–23
  changing structure of, 98, 132
  modeling, 31
  real-time analytics with, 33
  updating, 26
agile methods, 123
Amazon, 9
  See also DynamoDB, SimpleDB
analytics
  counting website visitors for, 108
  of historic information, 144
  real-time, 33, 98
Apache Pig language, 76
Apache ZooKeeper library, 104, 115
application databases, 7, 146
  updating materialized views in, 31
arcs (graph databases). *See* edges
atomic cross-document operations, 98
atomic rebalancing, 58
atomic transactions, 92, 104

atomic updates, 50, 61
automated failovers, 94
automated merges, 48
automated rollbacks, 145
auto-sharding, 39
availability, 53
  in column-family databases, 104–105
  in document databases, 93
  in graph databases, 115
  vs. consistency, 54
  See also CAP theorem
averages, calculating, 72

B

backward compatibility, 126, 131
BASE (Basically Available, Soft state, Eventual consistency), 56
Berkeley DB, 81
BigTable DB, 9, 21–22
bit-mapped indexes, 106
blogging, 108
Blueprints property graph, 115
Brewer, Eric, 53
Brewer's Conjecture. *See* CAP theorem
buckets (Riak), 82
  default values for consistency for, 84
  domain, 83
  storing all data together in, 82
business transactions, 61

C

caching
  performance of, 39, 137
  stale data in, 50
Cages library, 104

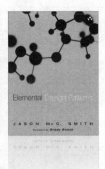